Teenagers and Attachment

Teenagers and Attachment

HELPING ADOLESCENTS ENGAGE WITH LIFE AND LEARNING

Edited by Andrea Perry

Sue Amey
Camila Batmanghelidjh
Louise Michelle Bombèr
Karl Heinz Brisch MD
Marie Delaney
Barbara Earl
Ann Heyno
Daniel A Hughes PhD

Foreword by Margot Sunderland D Litt

www.worthpublishing.com

First published 2009 by Worth Publishing Ltd
9 Charlotte Road, London SW13 9QJ
www.worthpublishing.com

Printed and bound in Great Britain by CPI Antony Rowe, Chippenham, Wiltshire

British Library Cataloguing in Publication Data
A catalogue record for this book is available from the British Library

ISBN   9781903269138

Cover and text design by Anna Murphy
Front cover image: Poppy Norrish

To Cara and Jonathan

Foreword

This highly original work on teenagers and attachment will be essential reading for any professional working with this age group. There has been so much written on the attachment needs of children, but this is the first book of its kind to address the attachment needs of adolescents. This serious omission in the literature seems to have been fuelled by common assumptions, held by many, that it is too late to address attachment needs at this age, and/or, it's just too difficult. The contributors show how misplaced such assumptions are.

Instead, the book demonstrates again and again that it is possible to successfully address the attachment needs of our young people, and that if we don't, we are likely to continue to see the same levels of teenage violent crime, depression, suicide rates, pregnancy and many other forms of disaffection as we have in our society today.

The contributors have all found their own highly individual ways of connecting with teenagers who are suffering from attachment difficulties, which have rendered these young people unable to learn, to relate in positive ways, to use life well. The contributors demonstrate how we must look further than the presenting behaviour of attachment challenged teenagers, and understand their presenting symptoms as communication of distress. From this standpoint, the contributors explain how to form a life-changing relationship with teenagers who are going off the rails, so that they can entirely change the direction of their lives.

Many of the contributors address the finer points of how to engage a teenager in meaningful dialogue, right down to the specifics of what to say and how to be. They explore how to listen, when for so many adults the pull is to talk *at* the teenager. They also discuss how to enable adolescents to feel 'held in mind', how to understand them and communicate that understanding, so that teenagers can experience the often profound healing of containment and accurate empathy. Moreover, due to the very considerable expertise of all the contributors, the reader can be assured that the interventions offered have been tried and tested over many years. There are also masses of moving case examples, which serve to bring both theory and practice to life.

In addition, throughout the book, the contributors offer vital clarification, using very accessible language, of the different forms of attachment styles and disorders and how each of these can be addressed. There are also particular chapters on how to work with a teenager's attachment needs in the context of the secondary school and also in supporting the teenager to make a successful transition to University. These contributions will be of particular value to the many secondary school teachers here and abroad who repeatedly experience feelings of failure, hopelessness and often intolerable levels of stress at work with these young people.

In short, the book will be a vital support, so that instead of fighting with adolescents or withdrawing from them, giving up on them or shutting down their own capacity to feel and think, professionals who work with troubled teenagers will feel empowered to engage and connect. In so doing the book will enable the reader to discover a strong and renewed sense of hope and vision in their work with these young people.

Dr Margot Sunderland
London 2009

Biographies
and acknowledgements

SUE AMEY is a UKCP registered Integrative Arts Psychotherapist, lecturer, teacher, dancer and writer. She has worked with young people in schools and colleges for twenty-nine years, with a special interest in working with refugees. As a performing dancer and writer, Sue embraces the arts as an instrument of healing and self-discovery. In her private practice, she offers family therapy and runs personal exploration and professional development groups in Oxford and abroad. She is also a supervisor.

Sincere thanks to my dear friend and colleague Doone for all her help and support in writing this chapter: Professor Alan Stein from the University of Oxford Department of Psychiatry: Linda Wisheart from The Children's Society: Group co-facilitators: Dr Flora Botica, Doone Elliott and Alex Barratt. Special thanks to group members whose poignant stories and courage have inspired us all.

CAMILA BATMANGHELIDJH is the founder of two children's charities - Place 2 Be, which now offers a national programme of emotional support and therapy in primary schools, and Kids' Company, which supports some twelve thousand children a year through a psycho-social programme of support. Camila describes her work as a vocation. She trained as a psychotherapist and is very grateful for the awards she has received but is too shy to list them. She does serious work but doesn't take herself seriously. She is the author of '*Shattered Lives: Children who live with courage and dignity*' (Jessica Kingsley Publishers 2007)

I am deeply indebted to the children and staff of Kids' Company for creating a community in which we have all learnt and can share our gifts.

LOUISE MICHELLE BOMBÈR is qualified as both a teacher and therapist. She has worked with individual pupils, classes, whole school settings, teachers and support staff across both primary and secondary phases. She has provided consultation to education, social services and health. She currently works as an Adoption Support Teacher Therapist for the Permanency Team in Brighton & Hove. She also works privately in therapy, clinical supervision, writing and training. She has pioneered her vision of getting lead attachment teachers and lead key adults into schools wthin Brighton & Hove. She is passionate about wanting to see pupils with attachment difficulties have every opportunity to access the wealth of experiences for relationship and learning in school, and is in the process of creating the evidence-base for her work with a view to influencing national policy on the treatment of children who have experienced relational trauma and neglect.

Acknowledgements to - Sue Darby - LAC Development Officer in Brighton & Hove, Lesley Torn - Inclusion Co-Ordinator, Sally Newman - Inclusion Co-Ordinator, Jenny Ansell - Mentor, Jody Monson - Mentor, Andy Schofield - Headteacher.

KARL HEINZ BRISCH MD is a specialist in Child and Adolescent psychiatry and psychotherapy, adult psychiatry and neurology, in psychosomatic medicine, psychoanalysis and group psychoanalysis, EMDR psychotherapist. He is also a specialist in trauma psychotherapy for children, adolescents and adults. He is Head of the Department of Pediatric Psychosomatic Medicine and Psychotherapy at the Dr von Hauner Children's Hospital, University of Munich, Germany. He is lecturer at the Psychoanalytic Institute in Stuttgart, Germany. His main research topic is early child development with the special impact of trauma on attachment processes and disorders. He has published on attachment development of high-risk infants, clinical attachment research, trauma, neuroscience, and written a monograph about the application of attachment-oriented psychotherapy in the treatment of attachment disorders. Visiting professorship at the University of Auckland/NZ. He is the German president of GAIMH (German-speaking Association for Infant Mental Health). He is the author of '*Treating Attachment Disorders: From theory to therapy*' (Guilford Press 2004).

I am grateful to Ken Kronenberg for his speedy and excellent translation, and for his cooperation over the past eight years. It is reassuring to have a translator who understands what you want to say and knows how to word your ideas. My three grown-up children, Verena, Nicola, and Jonathan were always in my mind as I wrote this chapter, because during their adolescence my wife Lizzy and I learned so much about attachment and separation from them and their friends. I want to express my very special appreciation and thanks for my wife Lizzy, who constantly reminded me that, despite occasional stumbles, we as parents were together creating a secure base for our children to mature, and to find their own ways to explore their world and take responsibility in their social relationships.

MARIE DELANEY is an Educational Psychotherapist, teacher and teacher trainer. She is currently living in Ireland and working with pupils and staff in a range of settings. These include secure units, alternative education placements, youth justice projects, mainstream primary and secondary education as well as private practice. She offers consultancy, training and workshops across the education, social service and youth justice sectors. She is particularly interested in bringing therapeutic thinking into mainstream education in order to help teachers deal with challenging behaviour in the classroom.

She is the author of *'Teaching the Unteachable: Practical strategies to give teachers hope and help when behaviour management strategies fail'* (Worth Publishing 2008).

BARBARA EARL is an English teacher and School Special Educational Needs Co-ordinator at Riddlesdown High School in Purley, Surrey. She has taught the full age and ability range for over thirty years and is at present managing the school's in-house support and inclusion project. Her prime interest is in working with colleagues to develop positive inter-personal relationships as pathways to emotional well-being and attainment for pupils. Her aim is to incorporate an Attachment-based stance both into her practice in the classroom and in delivering training in Special Educational Needs to Newly Qualified Teachers.

To my sons, J.J. and David, for inspiring me to learn and understand more about the value of

empathy in relationships. To the trainers at the Centre for Child Mental Health, where I was
first introduced to Attachment Theory and its implications in everyday life.

ANN HEYNO is an independent consultant and Commissioning Editor for the Journal of Psychodynamic Practice. She has been a student counsellor for thirty years. Until 2008 she was Head of canda (the Counselling and Advice Service)and Director of Student Support Services at the University of Westminster. She teaches counselling at Birkbeck, University of London, where she ran the Diploma in Student Counselling for ten years. Her background is in teaching and journalism, and she has contributed many chapters to books mostly in the field of student counselling. She is an Honorary Fellow of the University of Westminster.

I would like to thank everyone in canda, William Halton, Norma Gould and Colin Murphy, for
helping make my chapter possible.

DANIEL A HUGHES PhD is a clinical psychologist practicing in Annville, PA (USA) and specialising in the treatment of children and young people who have experienced trauma and attachment difficulties. He also provides family therapy based on a model described in his books *'Attachment-Focused Family Therapy'* (WW Norton 2007), as well as *'Building the Bonds of Attachment'*, (Jason Aronson, 2nd Edition 2006). Dan has developed a coherent model of treatment that relies heavily on the theories and research of attachment and intersubjectivity. He provides professional training throughout the US, UK, and Canada. *'Attachment-Focused Parenting'* is to be published by Norton in March, 2009.

I wish to thank Colwyn Trevarthen, PhD (University of Edinburgh) along with Allan Schore,
PhD and Dan Siegel, MD, both at UCLA, for their wise and comprehensive understanding
of human development which has served as the dominant guide for the therapeutic
interventions I have developed.

ANDREA PERRY practised as a dramatherapist in adult mental health for twelve years and was chairperson of the British Association of Dramatherapists from 1995 to 1997. She qualified as an integrative psychotherapist in 1996. She has provided consultancy within the private and public sectors, including collaborative family law, HR departments, the film industry, debt counselling servicess and the NHS. Her work on procrastination has been taken up by numerous UK university student counselling services. She commissioned the 'Attachment at School' series for Worth Publishing, and is the author of 'Isn't It About Time? How to stop putting things off and get on with your life' (Worth Publishing 2002) and 'Claustrophobia - Finding your way out' (Worth Publishing 2008). She writes for the national press and is a regular contributor to BBC radio on topics related to therapy.

I would like to thank Dr. Margot Sunderland, Graham Blench and the staff of the Centre for Child Mental Health: Dr. Heather Geddes: Susie Jackson: Griselda Kellie Smith: Roswitha Schmid: Alison Barty: the Tidswell-Norrish family: Anna Murphy for her marvellous design and enthusiasm: Martin Wood, Jenny Stacey, Geoff Pelham, Tsafi Lederman, Bruce Currie, Julia Waterfield and Jane Edington for their love and support; and all the contributors to this book, with whom it has been such a pleasure to work..

MARGOT SUNDERLAND D Litt is Director of Education and Training at the Centre for Child Mental Health, London, and Honorary Visiting Fellow at London Metropolitan University. She is also co-founder of The Institute for Arts in Therapy and Education, a British Accredited Higher Education College whose courses include Masters in Child Psychotherapy and Diploma in Adolescent Therapy. Margot has written over twenty books on child mental health, and her internationally acclaimed book, '*What Every Parent Needs to Know* (Dorling Kindesley), (the result of ten years of research on the long term effects of adult-child relationships on the child's developing brain) won First Prize in the British Medical Association Medical Book awards 2007 (Popular Medicine)

Contents

Introduction *Andrea Perry*   I

1   Attachment and adolesence - the influence   **9**
     of attachment patterns on teenage behaviour
     Karl Heinz Brisch MD

2   Survival of the fittest! - teenagers finding their   **31**
     way through the labyrinth of transitions in schools
     Louise Michelle Bombèr

3   How teachers can use a knowledge of attachment   **63**
     theory to work with difficult-to-reach teenagers
     Marie Delaney

4   Exterior fortresses and interior fortification   **97**
     - use of creativity and empathy when building
     an authentic attachment relationship in school
     Barbara Earl

(continues ...)

5   Principles of attachment and intersubjectivity   **123**
    - still relevant in relating with adolescents
    Daniel A Hughes PhD

6   Supporting adolescent refugees - developing a   **141**
    secure base
    Sue Amey

7   Terrorised and terrorising teenagers - the search   **175**
    for attachment and hope
    Camila Batmanghelidjh

8   Making the transition from school - attachment   **195**
    issues for adolescents going to university
    Anne Heyno

    Index   **222**

Teenagers and Attachment

NOTES ABOUT THE BOOK

1 To protect the confidentiality of individual young people, carers or professionals, names and autobiographical details have been altered in every case quoted. Any case examples written are composite and drawn from a number of similar examples known to the contributors from their experience over many years of working with children and adolescents.

2 To simplify the text, the male gender is used on occasion to represent the child or young person, and the female gender to represent educational staff. No prejudice implied by this.

3 To simplify the text, the term 'parent' is used on occasion to represent those now providing the primary care for children or young people. This term will therefore include adoptive parents, foster carers, family and friends

Introduction

Andrea Perry

> Primary school. I only just about made it there. Secondary school
> - well, this is a whole different ball game! My days are filled with
> so many moves and changes. I hate it. Each change presents me with
> yet another challenge. Another loss. Another opportunity to confirm
> to the world that I'm just as pathetic and useless as I first imagined.
>
> (*from* Chapter 2, Louise Bombèr)

Adults working with or caring for adolescents at school and in the community have one outcome in mind: to engage young people in the richest depths of experience life can offer. We want teenagers to have rewarding relationships and satisfying learning experiences, so that they can develop a confident and generous view of themselves, other people, and society, and look forward to their future.

But some adolescents, already struggling with hormones, physical changes, trying to be independent, and attempting to work out who they are and what they want, find it difficult or impossible to trust that adults genuinely have their interests at heart. When mistrust rules, the outcome can be chaos, conflict, misunderstanding and despair on both sides.

When children from insecure backgrounds become adolescents, they get bigger, stronger, louder (or more withdrawn), more aware of their needs, their abilities and their difficulties. The challenges they experience themselves and present for those around them can get a lot harder to sort out, before the young person can fully integrate into society. Such adolescents can quickly acquire 'bad kid' or 'anti-social' labels. They may form attachments by joining gangs, but in doing so, further alienate themselves from other more constructive options on offer. Lumped into an amorphous group by the media, written off and rejected as 'feral' or 'hoodies', they may see little option apart from living up - or down - to the negative images projected onto them by an increasingly wary community.

How can we help them? Can we have any hope at all of meeting them where they are, understanding their 'language', and enabling them to slowly build trust in us and themselves, and optimism about their future? The contributors to *Teenagers and Attachment* firmly believe we can.

Their belief is grounded in the extraordinary range and depth of experience they have gathered from working with teenagers in many settings. They have encountered young people whose ability to make healthy relationships and to find learning exciting - or even possible - has been severely compromised by their past experiences of trauma, neglect, abuse, loss, domestic violence or civil upheaval. The contributors have a profound belief in the capacity of authentic relationship to ameliorate early experiences of what they understand as *insecure attachment* (*see* p.10), into adolescence and beyond. Their ideas can offer hope to others on the 'front line' who may be feeling over-stretched and stressed, and want practical strategies that really work.

There is a sense that secondary schools can represent 'the last chance' for some adolescents, the ones with whom conventional behaviour management strategies just don't work (*see p.88*), for whom exclusion is a real possibility. This could be our last opportunity to recognise the needs which underlie their challenging behaviour. Misunderstood and left unaddressed, unmet early needs may drive the young person's behaviour in such a way as to lead him or her, in the adult world, into the arms of the criminal justice system, mental health services, or both. For example, thirty percent of children in custody have been in the care of their local authority[1]. Recent research shows that only six out of a hundred of this group will benefit from going to university (whereas in Denmark, six out of ten young people who have been care will do so[2]). These figures alone are an appalling indictment of the way in which we, as a society, currently treat the children and young people who have had some of the most damaging early experiences of trauma and loss. They should receive the best possible care. Everyone working in education has a real opportunity to make a crucial contribution not only to the lives of young people, but also to the creation of a more stable and safer society for us all. This book has been written as a direct contribution to that work.

Teenagers and Attachment is the third in a series of revolutionary books on working in schools with children and adolescents from an attachment perspective. The first book, *Attachment in the Classroom* (Geddes 2006), was commissioned at a time when, unwilling to condemn their pupils' challenging behaviour as simply 'bad', many in education were recognising the relevance of Attachment Theory (Bowlby 1953, 1973), especially when children's early experiences had led to the development of insecure attachment patterns of behaviour. By offering the key concept of the Learning Triangle (*see below,* pp.72, 81, 85, 199), educational psychotherapist Heather Geddes provides a straightforward way to understand how children's responses to difficult early experiences can fundamentally undermine their relationship in school to both teacher and task, leaving them so preoccupied with their distress that they cannot settle to learn. In addition, Geddes provides an 'attachment profile' for each of Ainsworth's three patterns of insecure attachment (1978).

These key tools have enabled education staff to recognise the particular behaviour and responses of their pupils with attachment difficulties, creating a starting point for reflection on how best to work with them. It has also given therapists and psychologists working in schools an attachment-based language with which to communicate with their education colleagues, a mutual perspective from which to view the pupil's challenging behaviour as a communication about their overwhelming and un-regulated distress. With warmth and clarity, Geddes describes the beneficial impact of a staff team collectively 'holding a child in mind' on the development of that pupil's capacity to retain his or her thinking when strong emotions are stirred.

The second book in the series, *Inside I'm Hurting* (Bombèr 2007), builds on this core understanding, providing a comprehensive treasure-trove of highly innovative and cutting-edge ways to work with these children and young people in our schools. Louise Bombèr describes how a relationship with a key worker as 'attachment figure' offers the child or young person with attachment difficulties an opportunity for 'second-chance learning', essential if that pupil is to be able to make the most of all that is on offer in education to develop their potential. Packed with practical ideas, this book has become an essential handbook for those wishing to understand what Bombèr terms the 'language' of insecure attachment, giving both the whole school and individual practitioners constructive tools for reaching and teaching children and adolescents who might otherwise be at risk of exclusion.

Both these books highlight the powerful impact on school staff of working with pupils with attachment difficulties. Dr Mary Bousted, general secretary of the Association of Teachers and Lecturers, commented recently that disruptive and challenging behaviour was an 'important deciding factor' when teachers consider leaving a school, or even leaving teaching[3]. The UK government has also noted the major challenges faced by staff working in secondary schools, even to the point of offering 'golden handcuffs' to keep the best staff in post[4]. Geddes and Bombèr recognise the high levels of stress education staff may experience, and strongly advocate the need for reflection time and support to be built in at a whole school level.

By containing the anxiety, frustration, anger and tension education professionals experience, the school is likely to retain the staff best equipped to contain their pupils' distress, establish constructive working alliances with parents and carers, and create the most rewarding and constructive learning environment for all involved. The language in the quote below indicates widespread recognition of the kind of support needed:

Schools in tough areas will always be fragile because of the social deprivation surrounding them, and so the support that they receive has to be consistent... the top priority is securing a stable and motivated staff.

Christine Blower, Acting General Secretary

of the National Union of Teachers (2009)[5]

Secure, consistent, stable - it's not surprising that such words crop up again and again within this book. They are amongst the key attributes of positive attachment relationships, on which so much that is life-enhancing can be built.

So *Teenagers and Attachment* has come into being as a direct result of teachers, SENCOS, psychologists, counsellors and therapists in secondary schools wanting more specific information about how to help adolescents with attachment difficulties, about what practical interventions work, about how to make schools into consistent, stable, secure bases for everyone there. Each chapter in this book has been written by a practitioner not only highly experienced in their particular field, but passionate about working with young people from an attachment perspective.

In the first instance, their work introduces us -

- to a core understanding of how patterns of attachment behaviour develop in children, and how issues which arise in adolescence, against a background of hormonal upheaval, are made more complex by the restimulation of earlier trauma and insecurity in young people with attachment difficulties and disorders (Chapter 1, Dr Karl Heinz Brisch)

The next two chapters identify the key challenges for young people with attachment difficulties within our secondary schools, and for the staff working there with them. Both chapters are full of practical strategies for working with these challenges.

They address -

- the impact of transitions to and within secondary schools on young minds already overwhelmed and preoccupied with what is happening or has happened at home (Chapter 2, Louise Bombèr)

- the different ways in which attachment difficulties will become apparent in the behaviour of the students in classrooms up and down the country, and how teachers can differentiate their approach to take this into account (Chapter 3, Marie Delaney)

The following two contributors take us into the heart of individual work with young people with attachment difficulties. They explore -

- the importance of using a 'light touch' in creating attachment relationships with young people, and the role creative arts can play in creating a bridge to the young person's world (Chapter 4, Barbara Earl)

- the relationship between attachment and intersubjectivity, and the crucial importance of playfulness, acceptance, curiosity, and empathy in the development of authentic relationships with adolescents (Chapter 5, Dr Daniel A Hughes)

The final three chapters illustrate work with specific populations of young people - refugees, teenagers in gangs and those pupils preparing to make the transition from school to university. These contributors introduce us -

- to creative ways of working with adolescent refugees and unaccompanied minors from an attachment perspective, using a group approach to create a secure base (Chapter 6, Sue Amey)

- to the world of the most alienated young people in our society, those who have experienced violence and may in turn perpetuate it through gang and drug culture; and to ways in which they too can be reached and offered positive attachment relationships (Chapter 7, Camila Batmanghelidjh)

- and finally, to the challenges and opportunities young people with attachment difficulties may face if they go to university, and what schools and colleges can do to enable them to negotiate the transition onward to independence, and into adult life (Chapter 8, Ann Heyno)

As Editor, it has been a great pleasure for me to get to know the contributors, and to 'hold them in mind' whilst they worked to convey their experience, insight and ideas. They are all engaged in generous and creative work, demonstrated by their real respect for the individual students whom they bring to life so vividly in these pages.

This approach is typified by Barbara Earl, writing about her work with a student displaying avoidant attachment behaviour. Feeling increasingly de-skilled in her work with Tony, a fifteen year old with an extremely disrupted family history, she accepts that if he could or would not learn, then she

"…had to assume that I had not yet found the right way to teach him"

(Chapter 4)

Such humility engenders a learning attitude on the part of the adult, and hope (that a way can be found). It leads to paths out of the impasse of failed intervention with adolescents, towards a feeling of competence and quiet confidence that however long it takes, a route and a point of contact will be found.

And the contributors' approach is characterised not only by their acute sensitivity to the traumas experienced by these young people, but also by their appreciation of, gratitude for and pleasure in those things about the adolescents they work with that are lovable, unique, amazing, funny, touching, inspiring and exciting. They are willing for the adolescent to 'move them' (Daniel A Hughes p.136), to affect them in positive ways, and are open to the adolescent knowing that he or she is having this impact.

Above all, the contributors enjoy teenagers, and they are not afraid to say so. They recognise, as Camila Batmanghelidj says (p.191), that -

> It is a privilege to work with traumatised teenagers. They have visited spaces of the soul which afford them extraordinary insight. Their courage and dignity is always deeply inspiring. Their honesty creates so much wonderful energy - and they will keep you young!

References

Ainsworth, M.D. S. et al (1978) *Patterns of Attachment - a Psychological Study of the Strange Situation* Hillsdale, New Jersey: Erlbaum

Bombèr, L. M. (2007) *Inside I'm Hurting: Practical strategies for supporting children with attachment difficulties in school* London: Worth Publishing

Bowlby, J. (1951) *Child Care and the Growth of Love* Harmondsworth: Penguin

Bowlby, J. (1973) *Attachment and Loss Vol II: Separation* London: Hogarth Press

Geddes, H. (2006) *Attachment in the Classroom: The links between children's early experience, emotional well-being and performance in school* London: Worth Publishing

NOTES

[1] *'Criminal Damage: Why we should lock up fewer children'* A Prison Reform Trust Briefing 2008 www.prisonreformtrust.org.uk

[2] *'Caring about Children'* Mark Easton February 3rd 2009 www.bbc.co.uk/blogs/thereporters/markeaston/2009/02/03/index.html

[3] *'Is £10,000 enough to keep me at this school? In a word, no'* Guardian Online January 13th 2009 www.guardian.co.uk

[4] *'Golden handcuffs deal for teachers in struggling areas'* The Guardian, London January 13th 2009

[5] Blower, C. (2009) *Lessons to learn if we are to get moving on social mobility* Tribune Online, 30th January 2009 www.tribunemagazine.co.uk/2009/01/30/christine-blower-lessons-to-learn-if-we-are-to-get-moving-on-social-mobility/

Chapter I

Attachment and adolescence

The influence of attachment patterns on teenage behaviour

Karl Heinz Brisch MD

Attachment develops in the infant over the course of the first year of life, and stabilises in subsequent years as an 'inner working model' of how to relate to others. This model determines how we enter into attachment relationships for the rest of our lives. Adolescence poses particular challenges for the development of attachment. It is a time when young people separate from their *primary attachment figures* - usually their parents - and seek out new attachments with peers and sexual partners. This separation or detachment is not without anxiety for the adolescent, which he or she will resolve in a variety of ways in new individual and group attachments, depending on his or her internalised working model of attachment.

In this chapter, I will first discuss the basis of the development of attachment and its significance for adolescence, as well as the various ways in which attachment may become disordered. I will then go on to describe the effects of such difficulties and disorders on the adolescent's attachment relationships, on her group attachments, and on her behaviour in the family and at school, in order to set the scene for the practical interventions described in subsequent chapters.

THE FUNDAMENTALS OF ATTACHMENT DEVELOPMENT

ATTACHMENT THEORY

Attachment Theory was developed in the 1950's by the English psychiatrist and psychoanalyst John Bowlby (1958). It states that infants develop a strong emotional attachment to a primary attachment figure (usually mother) over the course of the first year of their lives, based on a biologically rooted pattern of behaviour. If the infant or small child experiences fear (such as occurs when separated from the primary attachment figure), or pain, or external or internal threat, the child's 'attachment system' is activated in the form of an inner behavioural disposition. Depending on the infant's particular attachment pattern, he will exhibit different attachment behaviours in such a situation, such as clinging or protesting when separated. If the primary attachment figure is not available, *secondary attachment figures* such as the father, grandmother, or nanny may be sought out as a replacement. This ability to seek out a protective attachment figure is of lifesaving significance for the dependent human newborn and infant (Bowlby, 1975). No unlimited exploration is possible without secure emotional attachment (Ainsworth & Bell, 1970), which has clear implications for learning. For teens, exploration could be an excursion, or exploring feelings, ideas and thoughts about oneself or others, or expressing interest and curiosity in studying new topics at school (*and see below*, p.125).

If the need for attachment or the desire to explore are not satisfied, are ignored, or are acted on in a particularly unreliable or unpredictable manner, this may lead to ambivalent feelings toward the attachment figure, and also to anger, disappointment, and aggressive behaviours (cf. also Parens, 1993).

According to Ainsworth (1977), sensitive care-giving by the attachment figure, in other words, prompt, appropriate responsiveness to the needs of the infant, is crucial for the development of *secure emotional attachment* (Attachment type B). Mothers who themselves had a positive experience of attachment when they were children are generally better at this than are mothers who exhibit a more adverse attachment pattern, resulting from childhood neglect or trauma. A *secure attachment pattern* functions as a protective factor of resilience during later childhood development (Werner, 2000), and enables the child to better deal with emotional stress such as may occur when parents divorce. The development of *insecure attachment*, by contrast, functions as a risk factor, so that these children more frequently develop psychological problems when stressed or are less able to resolve conflicts in a socially competent manner (*and see* Chapter 6).

If the caregiver tends to reject the child's attachment needs, the child is more apt to develop an *insecure-avoidant* attachment pattern (Attachment type A). After separation, this child will be more likely to avoid the attachment figure or be less open to expressing his attachment needs. In extremely threatening or fear-provoking situations, these children will give up their attachment avoidance and turn to their attachment figure for help and protection, and she will then protect her infants.

If the infant's signals are sometimes responded to reliably and sensitively, but rejected or rebuffed at other times, an *insecure-ambivalent* attachment pattern may develop (Attachment type C). These children begin to cry loudly on separation and cling desperately to their attachment figure. They may also behave aggressively, for example by kicking their mother while seeking proximity at the same time. And they take a long time to calm down again.

Deterioration of organised attachment

A *disorganised attachment pattern* (Attachment type D) (Main & Hesse, 1990) is characterised by stereotypic and contradictory behaviour. After separation, the child may, for example, run toward his mother, freeze halfway, turn around suddenly, and run away again. Disorganised children tend to stop their movements, or 'freeze' for several seconds. These trance-like states are reminiscent of dissociative phenomena. When approaching their mother, these children can show clear signs of fear and agitation. It is apparent that their mother represents not only an emotional safe haven, but also occasionally a source of fear and threat, either because she responds aggressively to her child in attachment situations, thereby engendering fear, or because she herself responds fearfully (Main & Hesse, 1992). We see such behaviour patterns in mothers - but also in fathers - who have previously experienced trauma that they have not yet worked through. If one conducts an 'Adult Attachment Interview' (George, Kaplan, & Main, 1985) with such parents, they frequently report 'unprocessed' separation, loss or traumatic violence in their own childhoods.

The definition and classification of attachment disorders

At the far end of the spectrum of attachment difficulties, we see a variety of *attachment disorders* that can be traced back to more deep-seated changes and deformations in the development of attachment. These can be found in clinical samples of patients (Brisch, 2002). Before looking at how attachment difficulties appear in teenage behaviour in groups (*see below*, p.16), within families, and at school (p.19), it is important that these more extreme patterns are highlighted if adolescents in our schools are to be properly understood and helped appropriately.

What all attachment disorders have in common is an inadequate, contradictory or violent response from the care-giver to the child's early need for closeness and protection in threatening situations, or to the extreme activation of attachment behaviour in fear situations. This may occur, for example, when the infant experiences many sudden separations, or various forms of violence, resulting from parental overload or mental illness (Brisch & Hellbrügge, 2003; Brisch & Hellbrügge, 2006).

In situations that induce attachment behaviour, the disorders are so pronounced that they must be diagnosed as pathological. Two extreme forms of reactive attachment disorders can be classified and diagnosed in accordance with ICD 10* (Dilling, Mombour, & Schmidt, 1991 World Health Organisation), one form with *inhibition* (F 94.1), and one with *disinhibition* (F 94.2) of attachment behaviour.

*ICD-10: International Statistical Classification of Diseases and related health problems, 10th Revision 2007, World Health Organisation

Diagnostic classification of attachment disorders in childhood according to ICD 10

REACTIVE ATTACHMENT DISORDERS WITH INHIBITION OF ATTACHMENT BEHAVIOUR (F 94.1)	REACTIVE ATTACHMENT DISORDERS WITH DISINHIBITION OF ATTACHMENT BEHAVIOUR (F 94.2)
The capacity of these children to attach with adults is described as very inhibited. They react with ambivalence and fear to the attachment figure They exhibit an emotional disorder with withdrawal, over-caution, and an impairment in their capacity for social play.	Children show a diffuse, non-selectively focused attachment behaviour: attention-seeking and indiscriminately friendly behaviour; poorly modulated peer interactions; depending on circumstances, there may also be associated emotional or behavioural disturbance. Children with a disinhibited propensity seek contact without boundaries with the most varied caregivers.

Chapter 5, paragraphs F01-F99, Mental & Behavioural Disorders

Several other types of attachment disorders can be distinguished following and supplementing the forms of attachment disorders that have thus far been included in the international classification systems (Brisch, 2002). Clinically, these manifest as the children exhibiting *little or no overt attachment* (type I) and no protest on separation, even in extremely threatening or life-threatening situations. *Undifferentiated* - also called *promiscuous-attachment behaviour* (type IIa) - comparable to the diagnosis of F94.2 - is characterised by a lack of preference for a particular attachment figure.

Other children have a pronounced tendency toward *risky behaviour* (type IIb): they seek out dangerous situations and force their parents, other caregivers or medical staff into care-giving behaviour.

A further form of attachment disorder manifests as *excessive clinging* (type III). Such pre-school or school-age children require absolute and often very physical closeness to their caregiver or attachment figure to achieve peace and contentment, and are very hesitant to explore their surroundings playfully. They often attend neither pre-school nor school, and have few or even no contacts outside the family. In this type of attachment disorder, the children's fear of separation and loss of the attachment figure has become generalised and resembles generalised panic attacks, with a constant need for closeness and physical contact ('clinging'), even in older children. Their fear is thus more comprehensive and the need for closeness more pronounced than, for example, in children diagnosed with 'separation anxiety' (ICD 10 F93.0), as seen, say, in children with 'school phobia', which is a separation anxiety problem. Children showing excessive clinging cannot separate from their attachment figure even at home.

Being an attachment-separation issue, the term 'school phobia' is misleading, as it is not a classic phobia. It is similar only in the sense that the anxiety is projected by the child onto the school which is then anxiously avoided, as patients with phobias project anxiety onto an object or situation. Whereas children with an attachment disorder with excessive clinging seek out direct contact with their attachment figure to calm themselves, even in the home - a calm which they rarely find, in spite of closeness - children diagnosed with 'separation anxiety' exhibit a fear of imagined or actually imminent separation, but are able to function without anxiety in familiar surroundings.

The attachment disorder with *inhibited attachment behaviour* (type IV) (comparable to diagnosis F94.1 in ICD 10) manifests in over-conforming behaviour vis-à-vis attachment figures, frequently as a result of domestic violence. In the care of outsiders, such children are frequently less fearful and are able to explore their surroundings better. An attachment disorder with an *aggressive form of attachment behaviour* (type V) is an attempt to make contact with the preferred attachment figure. Unfortunately, she frequently responds with rejection, because she fails to recognise the child's concealed desire for attachment. As a result, the aggression-rejection pattern of behaviour tends to escalate on both sides.

Role reversal (type VI) can also be a form of attachment disorder. In such instances, children serve as a secure emotional base for their parents who may, for example, suffer from a chronic physical disease, addiction, chronic severe depression with suicidal ideation, or chronic anxiety disorder. The children themselves get little or no useful help in threatening situations, nor do they expect it from their dependent caregivers, from whom they then have difficulty separating.

Psychosomatic disorders with crying, sleeping, and eating problems sometimes develop in infancy in the context of attachment disorders. Pronounced psychosomatic reactions in childhood and adolescence are observed with attachment disorders, so that diagnosis and exploration of the inner working model of attachment is recommended where psychosomatic disorders are present, because attachment disorders may turn out to be the underlying condition (type VII). The diagnosis could then read: *Attachment disorder with psychosomatic symptoms such as eating disorder, bedwetting, sleep disorder.* The psychosomatic symptoms can also be coded as an additional disease that goes together with the attachment disorder.

The relationship between disorganised attachment and attachment disorders

Research indicates that there is a connection between disorganised attachment patterns in children and unresolved trauma in their parents (Lyons-Ruth & Jacobvitz, 1999). The child's behaviour, such as crying, may triggers the parent's memories of traumas they themselves experienced, because it reminds them of their own crying and their own pain. This, in turn, can trigger dissociative or trauma-specific behaviours in the mother or father, which, in turn, induces fear in the child (Brisch & Hellbrügge, 2003; Liotti, 1992; Lyons-Ruth, Bronfman, & Parsons, 1999). Similar interactions and psychodynamics may occur between teachers with unresolved traumas and their students. If 'pathogenic factors' such as deprivation, abuse, or severe disorders in the parent-child interaction occur either transiently or in phases, they may frequently be associated with disorganised attachment behaviour (attachment type D).

If, on the other hand, a pattern of neglect and violence, inflicted by the child's attachment figures beginning in the first year of life, are the predominant pattern of interaction, and if these pathogenic experiences extend over several years, attachment disorders are likely to result. These may continue even after a change in milieu in the case of adoption, with a better emotional environment, and are frequently an ongoing source of stress in the relationship between adoptive parents and child (Beckett et al, 2003; Steele, 2006). Attachment disorders often generate extreme distortions in behaviour that conceal children's real attachment needs beyond recognition and may, in the worst-case scenario, solidify into serious personality disorders, psychopathologies that may already be observable in adolescence (Brisch & Hellbrügge, 2003).

Attachment and groups

In addition to the dyad of child-parent attachment, children, particularly teenagers, also develop attachments to various groups that confer an important sense of security during adolescence, a phase of life in which separation is the challenge at hand.

Detachment or separation from the family is made possible by groups of adolescents that present themselves as a new and accepting 'emotional safe haven', in place of the security of the dyadic attachment (that is, pair-bond) represented by the primary attachment figure. Groups enable the adolescent to explore the world: enter, for the first time, into intimate relationships with others, and embark on other adventures, without necessarily gaining the consent of parental attachment figures. The young person's peers provide crucial support and encouragement. The feeling of safety in the adolescent group has a similar fear-reducing effect as did the sense of emotional security with the early attachment figure.

In *secure group attachment*, the group as a whole represents a *secure base* for the individual, which she can use in fear-provoking situations and as a basis for exploratory behaviour, either with the entire group or as an individual exploring the big wide world around her. She comes to feel that she can return to the group for support and security at any time, and that she will find acceptance there, which helps to defuse whatever fear she may experience. *Insecure-avoidant group attachment* occurs when the adolescent allows herself/himself to use the group for shared activities and exploration, but is fearfully reluctant to engage in emotional relationships within the group. *Insecure-ambivalent group attachment* is characterised by intense fluctuation between group activities and individual activities. When the individual leaves the group, she tends to feel insecure and then returns to the closeness of the group, resulting in ambivalent behaviour that vacillates between closeness to and avoidance of the group.

Psychopathology of group attachment

In *disorganised group attachment*, the group generates a lot of fear for the young person, while at the same time being experienced as less threatening than the dyadic attachment relationship. The group provides the individual with more potential for dissipating fear, but also more room in which to act, which is important for and used by adolescents developing a borderline personality disorder (all behavioural pathologies exhibited by borderline personality disorder patients may be seen in this context, including the potential for relationships with other group members or with the entire group to be broken off suddenly). Sexual relationships within the group and intense, even hostile, aggressive feelings and responses may be observed, in addition to the idealisation of the group as a protective, safe, and all-powerful place (Brisch, 2009; Brisch & Hellbrügge, 2009).

The seven types of attachment disorders described earlier may manifest in *disordered group attachment* in adolescents with, say, an attachment disorder with *inhibited* attachment behaviour: these teenagers not only avoid dyadic attachments and cannot use them for security purposes in fear-provoking situations, but they avoid groups in the same way. They fear them and withdraw from group activities, or never take part in the first place. The opposite is an attachment disorder with *disinhibited* (also called promiscuous or indifferent) attachment behaviour. Here, adolescents join numerous groups without apparent fear or difficulty, and switch allegiance frequently after only brief involvement. However, they fail to develop any sense of ongoing group attachment with a specific group. These adolescents are perceived by their peers in each of the groups they are in touch with as not actually belonging to any group. No group actually views them as members, nor do they themselves feel a specific attachment to any of the groups.

An adolescent with an *attachment disorder with risky behaviour* may become noticeable in a group in that the adolescent continually provokes accidents - either alone or with other group members - in order to gain more emotional support from other group members, who care for her as an accident victim. Young people with an *attachment disorder* involving *excessively active attachment* behaviour do not join groups in the first place, because they have a pathological attachment to a dyadic attachment relationship, often to their primary attachment figure, their mother. *Attachment disorders with aggressive attachment behaviour* are very widespread. Adolescents with this disorder tend, when afraid, to use the protection of the group to project their fear outwards, provoking people and picking fights, hoping to gain backing and support from the group (*see below*).

In *role reversal attachment disorder*, an adolescent - often a girl - 'mothers' an entire group and lovingly cares for individual group members, but is unable to accept help from the group when she is in trouble herself (*and see* p.24). This is a crucial difference between disordered and secure attachment behaviour; in the latter case, the adolescent provides protection and support to others in the group, but also allows group members to help her when the need arises.

Psychosomatic symptoms are frequent in adolescents with attachment disorders. To defend against anxiety, several adolescents in the group may develop eating disorders such as anorexia, obesity, or bulimia. Here, the anxiety of the individual adolescents is not contained by the emotional support of the group, but rather the group is held together by the symptom (for example, anorexia) and concern for the individual group member. All the members care for and worry about the anorexic in the group, and the adolescent experiences caring, protection, and support. So the symptom becomes persistent and no therapy can occur, because it would have to be sought outside the group. Rather, the notion becomes rampant that the group could actually cure the anorexic member. Group members collectively look for and fight those outside the group they deem to be responsible for the anorexia, such as the anorexic's parents or family of origin (*and see* p.25).

We will now look at how attachment difficulties and disorders affect the way in which adolescents manage the central task of adolescence - that of separation, within the family and at school.

Attachment, adolescents, family, and school

The attachment pattern developed during childhood determines the way in which an adolescent separates from her family during puberty and adolescence, and how she enters into relationships outside the family, including first friendships, intimate relationships, and group relationships with peers.

Securely attached adolescents initiate detachment/separation, and the discovery of new relationships and group identity during puberty, with relaxed curiosity, knowing that their relationships with their attachment figures are secure. Such adolescents develop stable new attachments outside the family system. They will be able to oscillate between familial and extra-familial attachments. They will enter into their first stable intimate relationships characterised by sensitivity and emotional availability for the needs of the other. They will be able to support classmates when they have academic or personal problems. In general, they will find success in school commensurate with their particular intellectual gifts and efforts, and they will enter into relationships with teachers and classmates that are characterised by mutual respect and cooperation. They tend to take responsibility in the groups to which they belong, including in school; are creative and flexible in their ideas for shaping the group; and find pro-social solutions in conflict situations that maintain the integrity and quality of the group. They are also apt to volunteer to speak for the group when necessary, without 'hogging the stage'. They place the goals of the group as a whole above their own narrow interests. They are respected and loved as well by their group mates as by their teachers, and can be very successful in life in personal and in academic achievements.

Adolescents with an *insecure-avoidant* attachment pattern tend to direct themselves outward and leave their family prematurely, either because they find it threatening or because they don't get the emotional support they need. They have learned to withdraw when in trouble, or to fall back on their own resources; in conflict situations they tend to respond aggressively with little thought about the social consequences. They do not prefer groups, and when they do join, their membership is shallow and lacking in emotional commitment because they expect little assistance from the group. They use their membership instrumentally to achieve personal or joint goals, but not for emotional support for the process of detaching from their families. If intellectually gifted, they are often academically successful, but they have trouble in relationships with people who have a secure attachment pattern. Problems may arise in early intimate relationships, when their partners express the need for closeness and support in moments of uncertainty.

Adolescents with an *insecure-ambivalent* attachment pattern oscillate between the desire for security in the family and the need to detach, needs they may have difficulty reconciling. They often accuse their family of trying to 'hold onto' them. But the truth is that their own confusion about whether to remain embedded in the family or stand on their own two feet is very great. Time and again, they try to gain entry to a peer group, but because of their ambivalence about their relationship with their family their peers often make fun of them for their 'dependency'. And so they only take part in the activities of the group half-heartedly, since they also want to spend time with their family. These two desires are often in conflict, and they accuse their family or their peers of attempting to stymie their development.

These young people may be quite successful in school, but they often fail to live up to their intellectual potential because they are still dependent on the emotional presence and support of their family and individual classmates. They frequently fear failure, and their self-esteem is easily upended. They look forward to school outings and being away from their family, but these occasions are often associated with anxiety and agitation. The adolescent fails to make a 'best friend' to help them endure the anxiety associated with the outing, as would be appropriate at this age (*see* Chapter 3 *for more on how both these patterns manifest in the classroom*).

Adolescents with an *insecure-disorganised* attachment pattern often show early signs of borderline personality disorders, much as they are seen in adulthood. Family members, friends, and group members find their behaviours and emotions hard to understand when the desire for closeness and help is at issue. Their reactions can fluctuate very quickly between seeking closeness and feeling stifled, resulting in belligerent accusations and even violence toward the group. The support they expect isn't enough, and they may suddenly withdraw, break off a relationship, express rage, or cry and whine like a small child. Occasionally, completely out of touch with reality or any actual incident, they may threaten suicide in desperation.

Because they continually 'make a scene', their friends come to see them as unpredictable (*and see* Chapter 8). Some of their peers may become intensely involved, but others may reject or ostracize them, express rage, or act out in other ways. Sometimes these adolescents actually manage to split groups. Splitting is a well-known means of dealing with anxiety in which, for example, group members may be split into 'good' and 'bad' friends. It often doesn't take long for the group to be split into members who sympathise ('the good ones') and those who reject the young person ('the bad ones'). In addition to shouting matches, actual fights are not uncommon. Similar scenes may play out in class with classmates and teachers. Academic performance fluctuates widely between good grades and bad - even if the student is gifted. Friends must constantly prove their allegiance, and the energy poured into shoring up the adolescent's attachment system leaves little over for intellectual exploration of academic material. The question that such adolescents ask each morning when stepping into class is not, *"What can I learn today?"* but *"Who loves me and will stick by me?"* Or conversely, *"Who do I have to fear; who is going to reject me?"* and *"Who do I have to I beat up before they get to me?"*

It is not uncommon for adolescents with attachment disorders to leave their families prematurely because they are subjected to violence, or to be removed from their families early by child protection services. They may grow up in foster homes or in institutions. Caregivers change frequently, as do the settings in which they are cared for. Relationships are frequently broken off, and their attachment system is constantly more or less activated. This means that they are actually seeking a secure attachment figure, but they are often unsuccessful in this endeavor because of the bizarre behaviour that results from their attachment disorder.

Adolescents with an *attachment disorder characterised by disinhibition* and promiscuous-indifferent behaviour will turn to almost anyone for help in fear-provoking situations. They seek out closeness without any sense of boundaries, including physical - and even sexual - closeness with complete strangers. They tend to leave their caregivers prematurely, and enter into relationships promiscuously. Often their caregivers are not their family of origin. They often trade sex for emotional attachment, security, and protection, with frequently-changing partners. They quickly enter into short-term relationships with other adolescents, groups, or much older adults - only to break off these relationships as quickly as they were formed. Other adolescents might describe them as not capable of relationships, or as 'superficial'.

Adolescents with an *attachment disorder with inhibition* in their attachment behaviour will often have been subjected to violence. This is why they tend to be very careful before turning to someone for help when they are afraid or anxious. They are unable to accept even well-meaning offers from teachers or foster parents and take a long time to develop trust, or to seek help in anxiety-provoking situations. They would be very hesitant to turn to a group of friends when they get into trouble. They tend to be distrustful of teachers and expect only criticism and belittling. They are often viewed as 'shy' or 'withdrawn' loners. In one extreme form of attachment disorder, adolescents completely avoid contact or closeness with others because their lives have been so traumatic. They also avoid groups, and live like 'lone wolves', in that they would rather hide and run away than seek help when they get into trouble. Contact with others triggers panic and flight.

Aggressive behaviour disorders are frequent in adolescence, leading to the question whether the need for attachment may not be behind the aggression. Such adolescents never simply go up to others and say *"I'm in trouble. Can you help me?"* Rather, they pick fights, both verbal and physical. Because of their own fears, they tend to use the group as back-up rather than accosting others on their own. Sometimes they are able to mobilise their entire peer group against an 'enemy' group, and even start brawls. When several adolescents with this pattern of attachment disorder with aggressive behaviour band together, they frequently form gangs that serve the purpose of protection so that each individual gang member experiences less anxiety - all of which is turned outward. Group loyalty is enforced absolutely, and this is the price paid for group protection. The result is pathological attachment to the group.

Any attempt to detach from the group activates fear in the other group members, so that the group will resort to almost anything, including violence, to enforce allegiance and prevent drop-outs. The real motive behind the aggression, however, is massive fear and an activated need for attachment to secure protection and help. Of course, this is desperately denied and defended against. The attacks on others are a displacement. Intimate relationships also induce anxiety. As a result, they are not even attempted, and gangs frequently develop into all-male or all-female gangs. Group alcohol and drug binges also serve to blunt anxiety. Sexual activity is not uncommon during binges, but it rarely results in intimate relationships, which would threaten gang cohesion. Only in therapy may adolescents come to recognize that their 'hard armoring' conceals a child's need for attachment, safety, and closeness. Only then can they open up for the first time about the violence they experienced in the home (Allen, 2002; Allen, Hauser, & Borman-Spurrell, 1996; Allen & Land, 1999). Often, these adolescents drop out of school and never finish (*and see* Chapter 7 *for more on adolescent gang formation*).

Adolescents with an *attachment disorder with role reversal* are often well loved. They cared for their nominal care-givers, typically alcohol- or drug-dependent parents, and functioned as their parents' secure base. In adolescence, they are prepared to take care of group members and intimates who are in trouble. They may also cook for everyone and make sure that the atmosphere in the group is conducive, thereby becoming the 'mother or father' of the group. They enjoy a particular status and get recognition, but never as much as they feel they should. As a result, they often suffer from feelings of guilt at not having done enough for the group. They then continue to sacrifice for others, with no regard for their own capabilities or their own needs. They find it hard to express their own need for protection and security, even in emergencies, and their friends are often left to 'guess' what they really need. They are equally well regarded in school, and often academically successful. However, their schoolwork may suffer under the internal pressure to care for others. They would rather help others complete their schoolwork successfully than ensure their own success. In their intimate relationships, they tend toward limitless care-giving, not infrequently ending up with alcoholic partners. This allows them to persist in their familiar pattern.

Occasionally, they are removed from their families in childhood by Child Protection services, because their own development is imperiled by their addicted parents. But more often than not they are left in these pathological family structures because Child Protection services understand that if the young person is removed, the family may deteriorate. This may constitute a form of child abuse on the part of the services, and in no way serves the needs of the adolescent. If they remain in the family, or even if they are taken in by foster parents, unless they receive psychotherapy, they will continue to feel responsible for their parents, siblings, or relatives, and they will feel guilty when they are unable to give them the assistance the family demands. They will make one attempt after another to return to their family of origin and stabilise it. It is not easy for them to enter into an intimate relationship as part of the process of separation, or to integrate into a group, because they constantly vacillate between caring for their family of origin, or their partner, or their own family, or the group. They frequently 'burn out' under this burden and become depressed, with exhaustion and physical symptoms (Yap, Allen, & Ladouceur, 2008, Yap et al, 2008).

All forms of eating disorders may be linked to attachment disorders and result from traumatic experiences in the past. This includes anorexia, which may result from long-term sexual abuse by an attachment figure. Such abuse often begins before puberty. Anorexia may be the only way that an adolescent - generally a girl - feels able to extricate herself from a pathological attachment - even if her self-induced starvation lands her in intensive care. The desire to separate and detach from a violently abusive attachment figure, but not necessarily from the family as a whole, generates a tremendous amount of ambivalence, which may be reflected in fluctuating weight losses and gains.

These adolescents generally do not join groups, but rather withdraw and spend many hours trying to control their weight. This strategy suppresses the anxiety that results from the violence experienced in the context of attachment. This form of control is often generalised to other areas in that the same compulsion may be used in the service of academic performance. Even if the student is not particularly gifted, she may get very good grades, but it will cost her hours of tireless, compulsive learning. Classmates frequently reject or tease such students as 'grinds'. But no-one senses the distress behind her starvation and her obsessive learning. As a result, she may become increasingly isolated in class, lonely and depressed, and sometimes even suicidal.

Prevention - an example of specific interventions

In Munich, our prevention programme, 'SAFE® - Safe Attachment Formation for Educators' (www.safe-programm.de), follows parents from Week 20 of pregnancy to the end of their child's first year of life. The goal is to teach parents in day-long seminars how to foster secure attachment in their infants. Parents who experienced trauma that they have not yet worked through receive individual trauma psychotherapy during the pregnancy, which begins with emotional stabilisation. After the birth of their infant, old traumatic experiences are specifically targeted for psychotherapy. The goal here is to ensure that these old traumas are not reactivated by the infant's behaviour, and that the parents are not tempted to respond violently to their infant.

Our experience to date has shown that the programme can break the vicious cycle of violence transmission from generation to generation. SAFE® mentors have now been trained in many countries (Germany, Austria, Switzerland, Australia, New Zealand) and offer SAFE® courses for parents.

If this programme becomes standard practice in the preparation of parents-to-be in these countries and indeed, more widely, we believe that more children will experience secure attachment with their parents, and thereby receive a stable foundation for the development of their personalities.

There are all kinds of overlaps between the different types of attachment difficulties and disorders, and patterns can be complex. An understanding of the importance of attachment issues can give us a starting place for recognising what young people's behaviour may be communicating, for planning effective interventions, and providing adolescents with appropriate support in our schools and communities.

More detailed descriptions of therapy for attachment disorders are found in Brisch (2002).

In summary

- Early attachment experiences have a crucial effect on later attachment behaviour in adolescence, both with peers in groups and intimate relationships, and in school with teachers and classmates

- The development of pathological attachment patterns, such as disorganised attachment and attachment disorders, could be recognised and treated in early childhood. Once they have become chronic in adolescence, they are much more difficult to treat

- The experience of new secure attachments however, can change the inner working model of attachment, even in adolescents

- Adolescence in particular is characterised by an increasing drive to find other and new secure attachment figures outside the family who may exhibit sensitivity towards anxiety and the need for emotional security

- All adults who work with adolescents, regardless of context, need to know about this opportunity

- Experiencing secure attachment in groups that are moderated by adults, and dyadic attachment with sensitive adults and/or adolescent intimates, may be sufficient to begin to steer the inner working model of attachment of an adolescent with attachment difficulties onto a new, more secure track - perhaps for the first time

References

Ainsworth, M. D. S. & Bell, S. M. (1970) Attachment, exploration, and separation: Illustrated by the behaviour of one-year-olds in a strange situation *Child Development* 41, 49-6

Allen, J. G. (2002) Psychoeducational Approaches *in, Traumatic Relationships and Serious Mental Disorders* (pp. 347-372) Chichester, New York, Weinheim, Brisbane, Singapore, Toronto: John Wiley & Sons

Allen, J. P., Hauser, S. T. & Borman-Spurrell, E. (1996) Attachment theory as a framework for understanding sequelae of severe adolescent psychopathology: An 11-year follow-up study *Journal of Consulting and Clinical Psychology* 64(2), 254-263

Allen, J. P. & Land, D. (1999) Attachment in Adolescence *in*, J. Cassidy & P. R. Shaver (Eds.) *Handbook of Attachment - Theory, Research and Clinical Applications* (pp. 319-335) New York, London: Guilford Press

Beckett, C., Castle, J., Groothues, C., O'Connor, T. G., Rutter, M., & the English and Romanian Adoptees Study Team (2003) Health problems in children adopted from Romania: Association with duration of deprivation and behavioural problems *Adoption and Fostering* 27, 19-29

Bowlby, J. (1958) The nature of the child's tie to his mother *International Journal of Psycho-Analysis* 39, 350-373

Bowlby, J. (1969) *Attachment and Loss Vol. I: Attachment* New York: Basic Books

Brisch, K. H. (2002) *Treating Attachment Disorders. From theory to therapy* New York, London: Guilford Press

Brisch, K. H. (2009) Bindung, Psychopathologie und gesellschaftliche Entwicklungen (Attachment, psychopathology and developments in society) In K. H. Brisch & T. Hellbrügge (Eds.) *Wege zu sicheren Bindungen in Familie und Gesellschaft. Prävention, Begleitung, Beratung und Psychotherapie* (Ways Towards Secure Attachments in Family and Society: Prevention, support, counselling and psychotherapy) (pp. 350-371) Stuttgart: Klett-Cotta

Brisch, K. H, & Hellbrügge, T. (Eds.) (2003) *Bindung und Trauma. Risiken und Schutzfaktoren für die Entwicklung von Kindern* (Attachment and trauma. Risk and protective factors in the development of children) (2. Auflage 2006 Ed.) Stuttgart: Klett-Cotta

Brisch, K. H. & Hellbrügge, T. (Eds.) (2006) *Kinder ohne Bindung. Deprivation, Adoption und Psychotherapie* (Children Without Attachment. Deprivation, adoption and psychotherapy) (2. Auflage 2007) Stuttgart: Klett-Cotta

Brisch, K. H. & Hellbrügge, T. (Eds.) (2009) *Wege zu sicheren Bindungen in Familie und Gesellschaft. Prävention, Begleitung, Beratung und Psychotherapie* (Ways Towards Secure Attachments in Family and Society: Prevention, support, counselling and psychotherapy) Stuttgart: Klett-Cotta

Dilling, H., Mombour, W. & Schmidt, M. H. (1991) *Internationale Klassifikation psychischer Störungen. ICD-10 Kapitel V (F). Klinisch-diagnostische Leitlinien* (International Statistical Classification of Diseases and Related Health Problems, 10th Revision, 2007 (ICD-10) World Health Organisation) Bern, Göttingen, Toronto: Verlag Hans Huber

George, C., Kaplan, N. & Main, M. (1985) *The Berkeley Adult Attachment Interview Protocol* (Unveröffentlichtes Manuskript) University of California, Berkeley: Department of Psychology.

Liotti, G. (1992) Disorganized/disoriented attachment in the etiology of the dissociative disorders *Dissociation* 4, 196-204

Lyons-Ruth, K., Bronfman, E. & Parsons, E. (1999) Frightened, frightening, and atypical maternal behaviour and disorganized infant attachment strategies *in,* J. Vondra & D. Barnett (Eds.) *Atypical Patterns of Infant Attachment: Theory, research, and current directions* (pp. 67-96) Chicago: University of Chicago Press

Lyons-Ruth, K. & Jacobvitz, D. (1999) Attachment disorganization: Unresolved loss, relational violence, and lapses in behavioural and attentional strategies *in* J. Cassidy & P. R. Shaver (Eds.) *Handbook of Attachment: Theory, research and clinical applications* (pp. 520-554) New York, London: Guilford

Main, M., & Hesse, E. (1990) The insecure disorganised/disoriented attachment pattern in infancy: Precursors and sequelae *in* M. Greenberg, D. Cicchetti & E. M. Cummings (Eds.) *Attachment During the Preschool Years: Theory, research, and intervention* (pp. 161-182) Chicago: University of Chicago Press

Main, M. & Hesse, E. (1992) Disorganised/disoriented infant behaviour in the Strange Situation, lapses in the monitoring of reasoning and discourse during the parent's Adult Attachment Interview *in* M. Ammaniti & D. Stern (Eds.) *Attachment and Psychoanalysis* (pp. 80-140) Rome: Gius, Laterza & Figli.

Parens, H. (1993) Toward the prevention of experience-derived emotional disorders in children by education for parenting *in* H. Parens & S. Kramer (Eds.) *Prevention in Mental Health* (pp. 123-148) Northvale, New Jersey, London: Jason Aronson

Steele, M. (2006) The 'added value' of attachment theory and research for clinical work in adoption and foster care *in* J. Kenrick, C. Lindsey & L. Tollemache (Eds.) *Creating New Families: Therapeutic approaches to fostering, adoption and kinship care* London: Karnac

Werner, E. E. (2000) Protective factors and individual resilience inJ. P. Shonkoff & S. J. Meisels (Eds.) *Handbook of Early Childhood Intervention* (2 Edn., pp. 115 -132) Cambridge: Cambridge Press

Yap, M. B. H., Allen, N. B. & Ladouceur, C. D. (2008) Maternal socialization of positive affect: The impact of invalidation on adolescent emotion regulation and depressive symptomatology *Child Development* 79(5), 1415-1431.

Yap, M. B. H., Whittle, S., Yücel, M., Sheeber, L., Pantelis, C., Simmons, J. et al. (2008) Interaction of parenting experiences and brain structure in the prediction of depressive symptoms in adolescents *Archives of General Psychiatry* 65, 1377-1385

Chapter 2

Survival of the 'fittest'...

Teenagers finding their way through the labyrinth
of transitions in schools

Louise Michelle Bombèr

The longer I work within education, the more aware I am of how crucial it is for us to reflect upon the journey that a young person with attachment difficulties makes throughout their life within the school system. From an emotional perspective, there is an increased potential for things to go wrong at secondary level: against a backdrop of trauma and loss, the mix of transitions and hormones can be disastrous. In the primary phase, any gaps between a child's emotional and chronological age can be managed fairly readily. However, in secondary, the gaps tend to widen, leaving young people with attachment difficulties more vulnerable to ending up on the sidelines. The secondary phase can then become a matter of survival. Who survives?

It seems that the fittest do. The 'fittest' seem to be the young people who have had 'good enough' early experiences (Winnicott 1964) and who have developed the emotional and social capacity and resources to manage the challenges of the secondary phase. But secondary schools are a minefield of transitions; between staff, peer groups, rooms and subjects. For a young person with an already fragmented sense of self - a consequence of relational trauma and loss - multiple transitions can be a recipe for disaster. Such young people can easily be left behind, misunderstood, and, at worst, excluded.

> Nationally, children in care are eight times more likely to be permanently
> excluded than their peers.
> Ofsted 2008, p.6

By 'relational trauma', I mean trauma experienced within a significant relationship - between a child and his parent or carer, through abuse or neglect of some kind. These relational traumas and losses can result in the young person presenting with *attachment difficulties*, an insecure way of relating to themselves, others and the world in which they live. It is important to emphasise that many young people with attachment difficulties have not simply experienced a single traumatic event or loss, but multiple, complex traumas and losses, often including numerous changes of care placements. It should therefore not be surprising that these young people find any kind of change difficult. Many have not had enough time or experience to consolidate a sense of stability from which to make sense of change. Many have significant developmental vulnerabilities that have not yet been addressed, leaving these young people at risk of being misinterpreted (Core 103, pp.6-7).

Change brings the possibility of new beginnings, which may be positive. But we sometimes overlook the inevitability of loss brought about by that change. Changes can also bring up anxieties about possible abandonment. Young, vulnerable minds may become overwhelmed with having to deal with all this, without the necessary ability to process what they are experiencing.

Who holds the young person in mind throughout transitions? Who co-ordinates and integrates the necessary support for them? Too often, the answer seems to be "*no-one*".

There is an urgent need for us to address these issues, and find ways to support the adolescents we work with. Our school system sometimes seems to perpetuate the cycle of rejection commonly experienced by these young people, rather than challenging or confronting it. If we could only recognise the power of relationship and stability, we would realise that schools really *can* make a difference.

A young person with attachment difficulties who has had the benefit of support in their transition to or within the secondary phase is more likely to enjoy their time at school, and be able to settle to learn. There is a then a far greater likelihood that they will achieve their potential emotionally, mentally and socially, which, clearly, will have a positive impact on the wider community and world of work. Greenlagh (1994) reminds us that we ignore the direct link between emotional growth and learning at our peril!

I'm aware that there is so much for us to learn, in order to become more effective in our ability to ensure that every young person, regardless of their early experiences, can make the most of all there is on offer to them within the secondary context. In this chapter, I will describe some of the principles I've learnt to date from young people themselves, and from the education staff who work with them, in order to achieve this aim. I continue to learn on a daily basis! Before doing so however, I would like to state what I believe to be the basis of all we are attempting to do with these young people in our schools.

Providing continuity, not 'fresh starts'

Our starting point with a young person with attachment difficulties needs to be their numerous developmental vulnerabilities. It is not sufficient to just *'leave them to get on with it'*, and then later pick up the pieces. However, a 'fresh start' is often introduced and viewed by many education staff as the appropriate starting point for the new year 7 intake, or within a managed move. This approach can have an adverse effect on those young people who have experienced relational trauma and loss in their early years.

When I began my specialist work out in schools, I observed how young people with attachment difficulties just about survived years 7 and 8 when they were *'left to it'*, and then noted how things seemed to fall apart drastically in years 9 and 10. It was heartbreaking to watch. I cannot stress enough how essential it is that we engage in preventative, supportive work with young people with attachment difficulties, regardless of whether they are 'acting out' their distress or not. The investment of our time, energy and patience with them in the earlier years will bring rich rewards by years 9 and 10. Our secondary schools are large communities of more than a thousand pupils; we shouldn't be surprised that vulnerable young people can become 'lost' from our minds. We must find ways to keep them 'alive' in our thoughts, so that we actively intervene on a consistent basis, rather than only reacting if there is a crisis.

In this chapter, I will describe the importance of preparation for transitions, and will outline the type of ongoing support needed to ensure these young people are well integrated into our schools. We will think through how to set up a secure base for the young person, through the provision of a consistent key adult and a consistent, protected physical space, well before day one. This is a must in the midst of a busy and often overwhelming secondary school set-up.

I will also look at the need to consider facilitating opportunities for 'translation'*, between the two 'worlds' of secure and insecure attachment. We need to see the behaviour of these young people as a means of communication. In fact, we may need to learn a completely new 'language', in order to make sense of what we observe in our interactions with these young people, so as not to leave their behaviour, attitudes and character open to misinterpretation. We also need to provide 'stepping stones' to help the young person to recognise the difference between how they have been relating from an insecure viewpoint, to how they could relate from a secure viewpoint, in the context of a 'good enough', generally safe school system; 'stepping stones' that can both match the young person's developmental stage, and make sense to them.

A system can easily be set up in school to ensure that education staff have the reflective space they need in order to make sense of the behaviour of these young people, and of their interactions with them, 'translating' what they experience as they go along. In other words, as mentioned above, the staff can be supported to recognise the young person's behaviour as the communication about distress it represents.

This can be achieved through TAC provision. A 'TAC' - Team Around The

*PLEASE SEE - Inside I'm Hurting, *Bombèr, 2007, Worth Publishing, p.8, p.97*

Child - is a group of staff who come together on a regular basis to reflect upon a young person's needs and his impact upon them. If TACs are not utilised, both the staff and the young people are set up for a rocky ride, and the risk of exclusions and/ or mental health difficulties may increase (*and see* p.53 *below for more on TACs*).

Planning transitions

Squeals and loud voices bounce off each wall along the vast corridors, making me jump inside. I am nudged and pushed out of the way as I attempt to get to my next class. I try to remember if it's week A or week B and whether I'm in P2 today or L35. Bewildered, agitated and hyper-vigilant, I arrive at the door of P2, hoping I've got it right.

A sense of relief floods through me, as there's Casey, my mate, chatting away to some other boys, so it must be French! Some familiarity.

Phew! However, I am confronted by another table, another subject, another face, another style of teaching, and yet another set of expectations. My body, which is getting bigger, feels awkward and clumsy as I push my way towards an empty chair. Grunts and sarcastic comments erupt as I accidentally touch others' equipment and bodies with my bursting school bag.

Over-stimulated and overwhelmed I attempt to make sense of a world really different to the one I've just emerged from. Primary school. I only just about made it there. Secondary school - well, this is a whole different ball game! My days are filled with so many moves and changes. I hate it. Each change presents me with yet another challenge. Another loss. Another opportunity to confirm to the world that I'm just as pathetic and useless as I first imagined.

The secondary phase is bewildering enough even for those from a 'good enough' background - never mind those who arrive with limited emotional reserves. What must it be like for young people attempting to negotiate another journey, a huge building, a range of lessons, a large community, differing expectations of how work is to be completed both in class and for homework, unfamiliar faces…? We wouldn't expect a much younger child, aged, say, six to eight, to try and manage this. Yet I would argue that some young people who arrive at secondary may well be functioning at this emotional age, due to the impact of their early experiences. It is quite common for people to become stuck at a developmental stage at the time of experiencing a significant trauma or loss.

With all this in mind, it is essential that we plan preparation work well in advance of the young person starting their new secondary school. Such planning should happen regardless of the circumstances or timing of this start. A young person may be moving up with their peers from primary in September, or may be moving mid-academic year because of a change in family circumstances, a change in their care or because of school exclusion. Whatever the reason, we need to take the impact of this major move on young people with significant attachment difficulties very seriously.

Unfortunately, however, we are often too quick to move young people around without taking the emotional impact of transition into account. As adults, we would expect a period of induction when we move job, considered by most employers and employees as good practice. Most of us have developed sophisticated frames of reference to work from to support us in our adaptation to the changes we are making. The young people in our care don't have such positive frames of reference, or experience, and yet are expected to just fit in and get on when they find themselves in a completely different environment. We forget that they are just like us in many ways, but with increased vulnerabilities. Young people presenting with attachment difficulties need access to a '…staged, intervention process, starting as early as deemed necessary' (Scottish Executive 2008, p.31).

PRACTICAL SUGGESTIONS

PREPARATION

Firstly, well before the young person's start date, time needs to be invested in giving the young person opportunity to think about the move, about the people, premises and environment of the new school they are going to. This might include giving them time to talk about their feelings about the move, and checking out the school's website together. Secondly, the young person needs to be supported to learn how to get around the new physical environment, and to become familiar with key staff. A member of staff from the primary phase needs to actually physically go with the young person to engage in these tasks together.

✔ **UNDERSTANDING THE PHYSICAL ENVIRONMENT**

"Help me get to know my new surroundings..."

It is wise to start checking out the physical environment of the new school from the outside in, and to do this in stages over a period of time. Give the young person ample opportunity to express both their hopes and their fears. Do everything you can to alleviate any anxieties by being explicit with your information-giving, to help put the young person at ease with this transition. Remember that these young people will appreciate the provision of more information, not less.

→ Collect maps

→ Take photos

→ Carry out orientation exercises to support the young person to find their way around

→ Buddy up with a peer from the school

→ Have lunch in the canteen together

Ideally, three or four visits are recommended, made together with a familiar adult from the student's previous school. The young person's previous key adult is appropriate for this role and responsibility (Bombèr, 2007).

Sudden moves, due to exclusion or a change in care

I would argue that such a move should be slowed down as much as possible. Remember that the young person needs support to make sense of what is happening. If a move is too sudden or shocking, then the young person will be forced to retreat into their most primary defence mechanisms, rather than engaging with higher level thought processes. I believe strongly that all transitions - even negative ones - have the potential to be a growth experience if handled well. Aim for a slow and gradual integration, rather than just expecting the student to get stuck in from day one. I would recommend preparation sessions as described below within a part-time timetable. Give the young person ample opportunity to build up to full time, and to full integration.

✔   CREATING A 'SECURE BASE'

A physical space   "I need somewhere to return to..."

Bowlby (1969, 1973) drew attention to the importance of children having a secure base for the best development of a healthy, secure attachment. This is especially relevant for those who have not experienced such security in their early years. Left unattended, these young people can become more and more entrenched in insecure ways of relating to themselves, others and the world in which they find themselves. A consistent 'physical' base needs to be identified. In the secondary phase, this is usually best placed within the inclusion department. At the end of each preparation visit to the school, support the young person to find their way back there. This is crucial when we consider how many different spaces a young person will have to negotiate during one day or within one week in secondary provision. We need to remember that for most young people, there will be twelve subject teachers, a form tutor, two or three senior managers and at least fifteen rooms/spaces to relate to and negotiate throughout each week. Having a secure base, where the student can be sure of finding familiar faces, will give him or her an anchor, enabling them to take the risks inherent in the transitions and the learning tasks they will encounter each day.

Wherever possible, use school staff to cover absent colleagues within the 'secure physical base', rather than agency staff, in order to maintain consistency.

An emotional secure base   "I need someone to keep me in mind..."

An 'emotional' base needs to be identified as well, in the form of a key adult (*see* OCDR 2007, policy 107). This should be a member of staff who is physically and emotionally available to take on this essential role, ideally for at least two/three years. The percentage of direct time spent with the young person needs to be matched to his or her specific needs and will reduce as they progress through secondary school. The more time that can be offered in the early years the better: such time will represent a real investment for the student's future years at school, both in terms of inclusion and in terms of learning potential.

We must be wary of only generating 'ideas' of support that present well in theory but don't actually have much substance in terms of practicality. These young people need genuine relationship, not merely a name on paper. From my experience, mentors and inclusion staff are best suited to working as key adults within the secondary context (*and see* Chapter 4).

Initially it is important that the key adult is chosen by the school. However, over time it is helpful if the young person themselves can be involved in the choice of who this person might be, from a select group of maybe two or three possible adults. For example, would a young person be better served by having a male or female key worker? Is there someone available who may be able to maximise any strengths or interests the young person has or would like to develop? The more opportunities of this kind that we can provide, the better: they will constitute a tangible commitment to the young person's future, both emotionally and socially.

Many need the opportunity to experience an adult initiating, taking the lead, offering, providing and maintaining 'good-enough' care. Let's not just allow these young people to continue on with what seems most comfortable and familiar for them, and easy for us. Let's overcompensate for what they have missed out on in their early years by giving them opportunities for 'second-chance learning'(Bombèr 2007, pp.299-300). In order to make and maintain satisfying relationships at school and beyond, they need to negotiate this stage of relative dependency, whatever their chronological age, since their early experiences were characterised by absence or distorted care. Let's be preventative.

To support the young person through any break before the move (for example, the summer holidays), encourage them to think of something small and tangible, representing themselves, that they could give to the receiving adult in their new school to look after. An example might be a photo, or a picture the young person has made, to enable the adult to keep the young person in mind (and for the young person to know they are doing so). Likewise, encourage the receiving key adult to give the young person something to take away with them, to keep during the break - a card, letter or photo for example. These so-called 'transitional objects' (Winnicott 1964) become very significant at times of major moves for young people with attachment difficulties. It doesn't matter if the young person loses the transitional object: what is more important is the symbolic representation imprinted on their mind. In fact, many don't lose them, as in the example below.

Ms Taylor (the primary school key adult) accompanied Dean on his transition visits in secondary. He was allowed to put up his picture in the Inclusion department and was given a card from his future key adult. As he was leaving the car park he picked up a shiny pebble and put it in his pocket, saying he'd put it somewhere special as it was from his new school. Ms Taylor writes:

"After the school holidays, I went to visit Dean to follow up his move. I was told by his key adult in his secondary school that he had settled in well so far. He grinned and pulled out the shiny pebble from his bag, telling me with great delight that he'd kept it safe and now carried it around with him. I realised then the importance of transitional objects for these young people."

These young people need someone and somewhere that can demonstrate that they are being 'kept in mind' during their numerous transitions. Someone who can hold everything together for them. Somewhere familiar they can return to. With this emotional scaffolding in place, the young person is more likely to have the confidence, courage and curiosity to explore and attempt new tasks and learning, out in the wider context of school. This relationship needs to be built upon and strengthened throughout the school year.

If we don't take the initiative, the young people themselves will often find alternative, unhealthy ways to attempt to satisfy their basic needs for safety, belonging and acceptance, which their experiences of deprivation have failed to fulfill. One way they may do this, often unconsciously, is by engaging in either avoidant or attacking behaviours, which may result in them getting themselves put on report. For a young person with attachment difficulties, being on report means that at least you receive some individual attention, on the principle that whatever attention comes your way is worth having, and better than nothing! Taking note of this, we can pre-empt potentially challenging behaviour by setting up an appropriate framework to meet these valid needs, through the use of 'check in' cards. These give the young person permission to meet with their key adult at certain points throughout the school day and week.

It is my experience that once staff have access to the practical strategies that are most effective, they relax into relating well to these young people. It is important that we learn to enjoy our students! The stronger and more positive the relationship/ bond between the key adult and young person, the more likely it is that the young person will be able to relax into their learning. If the bond is underdeveloped - or at worst, non-existent - the student may become preoccupied with the ins and outs of the dynamics between the two of you, and remain stressed.

✔   BUILDING A STRONG BOND OF WARMTH
    AND FUN TO FACILITATE ATTACHMENT

→   smile at and with the young person

→   Communicate your liking for him or her through the use of warmth in your tone of voice and in the words you use

→   Make the most of any opportunities to laugh with them, not at them

→   Find moments for fun together! It only takes two to three minutes to engage in a fun activity. Remember that some form of play at any age is beneficial

Smiling and laughing are by-products of a sense of comfort and safety. While we're enjoying ourselves dopamine is released, which impacts powerfully on the reduction of the stress hormone cortisol. Optimal levels of 'feel-good' brain chemicals mean more potential for forming important new synaptic connections key to the capacity to learn and enjoy learning. (Sunderland, 2006). Fantastic news for schools!

✔   FILES *"Remember my starting point and how far I've come..."*
I was concerned to hear about Kim, who is a looked-after young person with a complexity of relational traumas and losses to date. The Deputy Head of Kim's secondary school called me over as he noticed me heading off down the corridor for a meeting...

"Kim has just arrived here from _____ authority. She has been fostered by carers here. We don't know anything about her yet as the files still

haven't arrived. Not to worry, she seems okay. We got her integrated in
as soon as she arrived, and she's been no trouble yet. She seems quite
quiet and compliant so I don't think we'll have any issues there!"
  The files arrived after about six weeks.

It is essential that necessary paperwork arrives *before* the young person does, and that it is read! Do everything you can to communicate how crucial it is that you have access to this information, and if you can't get hold of the paperwork, demand a meeting with either the social worker or with a member of the education staff from the previous authority. I've been concerned when members of staff declare triumphantly that they don't want to pre-judge a young person by reading too much about them. It's a good job that doctors don't engage with this practice in hospitals, or we'd be in trouble! This thinking has got to be challenged for young people who are vulnerable to being misunderstood or overlooked. They need consistency and a seamless approach - not fresh starts. If we were to track their personal histories, we would probably find that they were all too familiar with making many stops and starts in their short lives to date. They need the experience of stability; schools are extremely well-placed to offer this. The following words really sum up the type of provision we need to be facilitating for young people with attachment difficulties in our schools.

Stable: *abiding, constant, durable, enduring, established, fast, firm, fixed, immovable, invariable, lasting, permanent, reliable, secure, sound, steadfast, steady, strong, sturdy, sure, well founded*
  Thesaurus - HarperCollins Publishers, Glasgow (1994)

Experience indicates how important it is for young people with attachment difficulties to remain in their schools wherever possible, despite changes in their family situations. As education staff, we must recognise the importance of maintaining the continuity of care we provide, making the most of every opportunity to create stability.

In my work with schools, I have been advocating the use of a confidential A4 factfile at the front of a pupil's file. This can be used at times of transition as a quick reference point, as we need to be realistic about what we can manage ourselves in the busy-ness of moves and transitions. I recommend that the following key information is included on this factfile:-

> → a summary of the young person's relational traumas and losses
>
> → a list of known triggers (for example, a shut door, a sudden noise, raised voices and so on*)
>
> → an outline of strategies that are known to be effective in helping the young person settle to learn

This needs to be a working document, one which is updated from time to time as the young person is 'learned' by the core staff working with him or her (Cairns, 2004).

A caveat about confidentiality

Information in this factfile should be only shared on a 'need to know' basis. The key adult and a member of senior management both need access to the finer detail. Subject teachers only need an overview. Young people themselves have commented that they do not want everyone knowing their business, and we need to honour and respect that (*see* OCRD 2007, policy 104).

Those of us who do have access to information about a young person need to be mindful of not making negative or unhelpful judgements. We need to remember that every young person is capable of adaptation as each day goes by. We need to remember that none of us have life sentences over our heads, despite being reminded

---

TRIGGERS: *These small stimuli can repeatedly set off the same level of stress response from the young person that they originally experienced in response to an unsafe situation, just as a soldier traumatised by gunfire may respond to a car backfiring by rushing to take cover.*

of our inadequacies from time to time! It is essential that we hold onto hope and high expectations for each young person with whom we work, as this has an impact on all the young person might become.

> Treat people as if they were what they ought to be and you help them become what they are capable of being.   Goethe, J. (1749-1832)

✔   MAKING ENDINGS POSITIVE

"I might mess up but please don't forget that I'm human too"

Regardless of the circumstances, if a young person has to leave our particular school, we do need to pay attention to how this is managed and we need to ensure that we include the young person in planning for the departure (*see* OCRD 2007, policy 105).

> *"Gary completely lost it one day, and grabbed a rolling pin in the food technology lesson, threatening to hit someone with it. The class was removed from the room and Gary was then calmed down by two senior managers. Gary usually seemed like a reserved, compliant young man, but something had been really bothering him lately. I was aware that he was in care due to having witnessed significant domestic violence in his birth family and that he'd been having flashbacks despite now living in a safe home. We never saw him again. He merely disappeared. After about a week I found out he'd been excluded. All his classmates had been asking about him and I wasn't quite sure what to say to them".*
>
> (Food Technology Teacher)

Exit procedures need to be thought through if the young person is to learn from the process, rather than simply experience it as yet another traumatic rupture. It is so important that a young person has a positive send-off wherever possible, no matter what has happened. If possible, they need to be given some quality one-to-one time well after a situation has calmed down. We need to ensure that they have some sense of the truth of why they are going, be given opportunities to say their goodbyes, and for those closest to them to say their goodbyes too.

This may well be the first time in the young person's life that a fraught ending has been handled well by mature adults, so we need to make the most of the possibility of giving them a different experience of what life can be like. Our choices are crucial. I feel we are often unaware of the huge responsibility we carry for the effect we may have on the future emotional and mental health of a young person with attachment difficulties. The way in which situations (such as endings) are handled has the potential to be reparative. They can become educative opportunities for developing the student's sensory, emotional and social literacy. If handled wisely, a weakness or vulnerability can be shifted into an opportunity for growth. To do this well demands reflection, and so schools need to allow staff the opportunity and quality time to reflect and to seek advice from outside professionals - particularly those with an expertise in relational trauma and loss, for example community mental health workers, psychologists, therapists and so on.

Another type of ending also requiring specific attention is that of the young person suddenly being removed from school due to a change in care arrangements. Staff and the student's peers can arrive back after a weekend or extended break to discover that a young person has 'disappeared'. I would strongly advocate that education staff take action and follow up what has happened to the young person. Too often we settle for *"That's just the way it is"*.

> Significant transitions which did not take place at normal transition points between primary and secondary or secondary and post school were not uniformly managed with the required care and attention.
>
> Scottish Executive, 2008

Visit the student at least once as a follow-up if at all possible, and inform his peers as to where he is and how he is doing. Organise a goodbye card, photo, gift and so on from his form group and the education staff involved. Let's remember that young people with attachment difficulties have feelings and that relationships do matter to them - even if they don't always show that in the way we might be familiar with. Let's make all transitions positive as an investment in young futures.

SUPPORT PROVISION FROM DAY ONE

✔   MEET AND GREET

"I need opportunities for continuity and certainty..."

'Meets and greets' in the morning are significant. In good primary schools this happens as part of the usual daily routine. We need to be aware that a young person who has attachment difficulties could well arrive in school 'all over the place'. He may have had contact with his birth family the night before, had control battles with his adoptive parents at breakfast, packed week A's books instead of week B's books, and then arrived in your classroom completely preoccupied - with learning nowhere on his agenda! An opportunity for 'grounding' is helpful preparation for the young person and is an investment for a productive day for the education staff too - believe me!

It is helpful if the young person can have access to the inclusion department first thing in the morning, to see their key adult and to get organised for the day before joining their class for registration. Good practice would include saying hello by name, asking a couple of exploratory questions in order to help the young person process what has happened prior to arriving at school, and guiding them toward their own tray/locker provided to help them keep their things organised. This would be more common in the primary phase, but will also be of significant value in secondary.

It may seem surprising that this should be necessary. But we need to remember that young people who have experienced relational trauma and loss in their early childhood often need further opportunities to re-visit and consolidate far more experiences and developmental stages from their primary school days than we might imagine, as there are usually gaps in many aspects of their development (*see below*, p.52). The key adult is best placed to track the progress and whereabouts of the young person, especially during the first weeks and months. Round-robins distributed to staff can be used to collect information about the young person's strengths and weaknesses, providing key workers with a good overview of school life for the young person in their care.

✔ KEY MESSAGES

"I need you to remember that I don't make sense of the world
the same way you do..."

It is crucially important that certain key messages are communicated at every opportunity throughout a young person's journey through school life. Some examples will include:

> *"**Safety** is a priority in our school".*
>
> *"There are **enough** resources for you to do your work".*
>
> *"You may feel fear and panic inside from time to time but we are going to **help you practise taking control of those feelings** so you don't get overwhelmed."*
>
> *"Even though there are a few of us that work with you in this school, we all talk and share ideas of how to support you best, **as we are for you**."*

These messages should be communicated through both words and actions. Be as explicit as possible. These young people need such repetition in order to form new neural pathways and networks (Sunderland 2006) - helping them make new meanings for the world they now find themselves in. School can represent a world of security and stability. If we don't recognise this need for new, explicit, key messages, these young people will return time and time again to old, internal 'scripts' that were helpful for living in an unsafe, insecure, unstable environment, but are not helpful now and/or within the context of school.

✔ ORGANISATIONAL SUPPORT

"I need you to model to me how to get organised, as I learn that through others..."

Many young people with attachment difficulties have difficulties with organisation. The key adult can teach them a huge amount by merely modelling, in an explicit way, how they themselves get organised, through the use of commentaries (Bombèr, p.96). I advocate shadowing work that the young person has to complete from time to time, so that they can see how you attempt tasks and challenges.

Mobile phone alarms or stop-watches are helpful when a young person needs to be somewhere at a certain time. Support him or her by setting up reminders. Let's take away the pressure of having to remember, so that there's one less thing for them to have to think about.

✔ REGULAR TIMETABLED SUPPORT

"I will need extra time and support as I have so much to catch up on..."

At least one lesson a week needs to be identified for the young person to visit the inclusion department and check in with their key adult. The type of work done in this lesson will vary depending on the needs of the young person, but a usual slot might consist of some identity work, social skills practice, organisational skills support and curriculum catch-up (*see* Kelly 1997, 2003, 2004, & Morgan 2007).

✔ CHECK-INS

"I will need reassurance that you're still there, keeping me in mind..."

It is important that the young person has the flexibility and freedom to 'check in'. By allowing this, we will be providing them with an opportunity to practise relative dependency, a pre-requisite to independence. As mentioned above, this 'anchor' provides the necessary security a young person needs to negotiate other challenges that they may not yet be quite ready for developmentally.

It is not helpful if the inclusion department has a rigid entry policy! Yes, some young people may misuse this facility. But rather than restricting access to all because of this minority, let's set up alternative plans for the ones unable to use such support appropriately, and allow the young people with attachment difficulties access in order to thrive. Many young people with attachment difficulties need somewhere to check in as part of their support requirements, and so it's important to think through how this can be catered for.

✔   OTHER SPECIAL NEEDS PROVISION

"Don't let me get overwhelmed with too much..."

Some young people, especially those who have experienced severe neglect in their early years, may need a number of different types of support provision, in addition to the regular school timetable. With this in mind, it is essential that the key adult takes the lead in integrating any advice from external services/agencies into a support plan that will involve the minimum of transitions. We need to remember that for young people with an already fragmented sense of self, integrated support is the recommended route towards inclusion, rather than sending them off for numerous discrete support provisions during the school day (*and see* p.97). This is even more important during adolescence, as the young person will be very conscious of somehow being able to 'fit in' with their peer group.

An example of bad practice

'Liza has -

Ms Bebbs for literacy support on Mondays period 3 week B

Mr Patel for numeracy support on Wednesdays period 4 week A

> *Mr Rigs for keyboard skills on Fridays half way through period 1 in week A for thirty minutes*
>
> *Ms Sharpe for speech and language support on Thursdays period 2 week B*
>
> *Ms Beattie (Key adult) individual session on Wednesdays period 2 each week A & B'*

I expect that this insert in Liza's school planner is as confusing to you as it was to me. However, this is common for some young people with attachment difficulties out there to try and make sense of and manage! These young people may well need all this additional support, but let's think through how to integrate their experiences in schools in a more manageable way. Ideally this support should be delivered through the key adult's relationship and individual, direct time with the young person. However, if that's not possible for whatever reason, then the rule to be borne in mind is the need for fewer adults and fewer changes of space.

✔ HOME/SCHOOL PARTNERSHIP

"Keep together. Keep talking."

Home/school partnership tends to drop off as the young person moves into the secondary phase, but this needs to be re-instated as a matter of priority. Be wary of numerous members of staff liaising with parents or carers when supporting young people with attachment difficulties. The potential for splitting* is far greater for young people such as these. Subject teachers need to be informed that the key adult is to take the role of gatekeeper for any information that needs to be shared, to avoid this happening.

__SPLITTING__ is an unconscious defence mechanism used against anxiety, whereby a 'Jekyll and Hyde' dynamic occurs - of people viewing themselves, that is, 'us', as 'all good', and other people, that is, 'them', as 'all bad': promoting division and blame, and reducing the possibility of a mature overview of difficult situations from all concerned (and see Chapter 1 p.21).

It is advisable for the key adult to communicate with the parent or carer weekly, co-ordinating information given by different subject teachers as and when deemed appropriate. Email communication is usually the preferred medium of contact, due to logistics in secondary schools, although this may not always be appropriate for every family. It is sometimes important to put boundaries around home/school communication, limiting both key adult and the parent or carer to two or three bullet points and trying to balance out what is shared by including both strengths and weaknesses. This boundary setting can be important, as both parties can otherwise end up writing essays for many reasons, including managing their own anxiety, and this can then become unmanageable!

As education staff, we do need to be very mindful to include positive points regardless of how we've experienced the young person personally. Simply describing all their failures and weaknesses is not good practice. Let's think about how we communicate different information to young people and their parents/carers. It is much more helpful to describe someone needing 'to practise' or 'get stronger at' something, than simply stating that they can't or won't do it. The former language suggests the hope and expectation of progress!

GETTING ALL THE STAFF ON BOARD...

✔   DEVELOPMENTAL VULNERABILITY

"It will take me a longer while to catch up with myself,

so don't be fooled by my age."

From day one, we need to ban the phrase "*At this age you should be...*". This is really unhelpful. Many of these young people are likely to have a developmental vulnerability - meaning that their behaviours can be indicative of those more commonly associated with younger emotional and social ages. This can set them apart from their peers. This must be our starting point - not their chronological age. This understanding or insight can be communicated through staff briefings, round-robins or through staff noticeboards/books. We need to differentiate our emotional and social expectations of them in line with this information, as we would as a matter of course for the rest of the curriculum.

We are responsible for making the most of what we know. We need to remember that for young people who have experienced so much relational trauma and loss there are bound to be delays in progress, and that this is okay! Some deserve a medal for even getting themselves into school, never mind being able to negotiate the other challenges ahead of them as well. Remember it will take longer to learn later what the brain was designed to learn at a much younger age, as the brain is not growing as rapidly now as it was in the young person's early years. We know for ourselves that learning new skills gets harder as we get older. Let's honour and respect the physiological pace our students need, rather than demanding the impossible.

✓ CONTINUING PROFESSIONAL DEVELOPMENT
   "Keep yourself up to date with the latest research,
   as I deserve the best support..."

Staff need to be encouraged to access information on attachment difficulties through reading, training and meeting with outside agencies. Whatever the curricular focus, the emotional and social developmental age of the pupil needs to be reflected upon, as this will enable us to plan appropriately. We have a responsibility to differentiate for the young people in our care.

✓ TACS
   "Look after one another well so you can look after me..."

The key adult needs to take the lead in facilitating a TAC (Team Around the Child) - a preventative, protected, reflective space for internal school staff to consider the young person and to plan consistent ways of interacting with them. Integrated support is necessary. A TAC is supervised by someone with clinical expertise, so that any anxiety that staff are experiencing about the particular young person can be contained, and concerns managed appropriately. I recommend that a counsellor/ therapist is best placed to take on this role of supervision. He or she needs to be someone from outside the school (not the school counsellor). Some secondary schools choose to pair up with other schools in their area and swap their school counsellors/therapists for the purpose of TACs.

Heightened levels of anxiety are inevitable when relating to those who have experienced trauma and loss. If TACs are not facilitated, then the young person can become at risk of being misunderstood, since many of their behaviours could be easily misinterpreted by others as 'bad' or 'mad'. For too long we have expected education staff to merely supervise one another. This would be fine if we weren't relating to some young people with significant attachment difficulties in our schools. As education staff, we are vulnerable to secondary stress symptoms as a result of our contact with young people who have had extremely difficult early experiences. We can't completely protect ourselves from the impact on us. This is therefore an important emotional and mental health and safety matter that needs to be addressed appropriately. I would recommend that meetings such as these are viewed as integral to school systems. There needs to be space within schools for opportunities for translation (*see above*) and for thinking through the psychological processes that are inherent within experiences of relational trauma and loss.

> *"TACs make staff stop and think. They empower staff to feel that they are not on their own. We all benefit from collective contributions, enabling staff to be more consistent in their approach, language and expectations".*   (Inclusion Co-Ordinator)

> *"In my other school I was working with a young person in care and nearly got burnt out. I was so encouraged to find that this school ran*

TACs. It is clear they take the mental health of both the young people in the care and their staff seriously". (Key Adult)

✔ PROMOTING DIGNITY

"I will need your advocacy as I'm so easily misunderstood..."

I believe that we should have guidelines or a policy that maps out what is expected of staff to promote dignity in schools. You may wonder why this is necessary. Over the years, regrettably, I - I'm sure like you - have heard and been profoundly shocked by language used to describe vulnerable young people, and witnessed behaviour from particular staff members that should have resulted in disciplinary action, but which has been overlooked.

Natasha's moment of toxic shame

Natasha was pointed out in front of the whole assembly gathering as she was fidgeting*.

She was sternly told to stand up and to stand on a line. She was then told to move a little to the left and then to the right. Natasha felt intimidated and humiliated by the member of staff who was wielding a great deal of power in that moment. She ran out of the hall into a nearby classroom - probably to hide and take time out. However, she was followed by three senior managers, who surrounded her, shouting and physically closing in on her, arms wide open as if to catch her.

"You need to sort yourself out Natasha ... you're such an idiot ... you won't amount to much the way you're going!". "Stupid girl ... just calm down and do as you're told". Natasha started screaming hysterically and hitting out at them. One of the staff got caught on the arm. Natasha was immediately excluded.

I believe that we need some kind of framework that provides guidelines to protect young people who are known to be vulnerable. We need to be so careful in our choice and use of language and behaviour when relating to them, because what we say and do will have a profound effect on them. Yes, these young people are more likely to tap into our personal vulnerabilities than almost any others. Nonetheless, we have to maintain our ability to behave professionally. If we need support, we need to keep asking for it until we get it. Whatever we feel at the time, we all know that it is unacceptable to take out our frustrations on the young people with whom we work; they are the reason we have employment. We are there to work amongst them.

Schools do need to get better at looking after their staff, by being more aware of the secondary stress symptoms that can be set off when relating to those who have experienced relational trauma and loss. But regardless of how good, bad or indifferent our school is at supporting its staff, we all have to take responsibility for promoting dignity in all we communicate to these young people. The more challenging the circumstances, the more opportunity for us to be modelling containment of anxiety and tension, or for coming up with ideas for good practice.

✔ DIFFICULTIES WITH STUDENTS

**"I can quickly become overwhelmed with fear, panic and shame. Help me
to keep thinking by teaching me how to keep my anxiety levels down."**

It is important to have an action plan drawn up if a pupil is known to act out some of their distress in school. At times of difficulty, it is essential that fewer adults are involved than is usual practice in secondary schools. In my experience in schools, a pre-existing plan that indicates which specific members of staff from senior management will deal with particular students has been helpful. Whenever

Many young people who have experienced trauma and loss are unable to sit still due to the level of stress in their bodies - a physiological response.

possible, it is important to have the young person's key adult present for whatever conflict resolution is needed. They can provide the necessary 'translation' for the pupil and follow up on whatever reparation or communication is necessary (here, 'translation' would mean providing an understanding of the situation, unpicking both the young person's interpretation of what happened or was experienced, as well as the interpretation of the other people involved). How these difficulties are dealt with is so important. The language used must be thought through. Anything that might induce shame needs to be kept to a minimum, so that the young person is freed up to keep thinking. This is because young people who have experienced relational trauma and loss have high levels of shame already, and so additional shame can become toxic for them and overwhelm their capacity to think.

In conclusion

It is a fact that secondary schools, set up as they are now, are places that are best negotiated by the emotionally and socially 'fittest' of our young people. Those who have significant attachment difficulties and developmental vulnerabilities are therefore very much at risk within our current systems. There is so much we can do to either make or break these young people's experience of school. If we don't pay attention to their additional needs by providing appropriate support in schools, then both the young people themselves and we will pay the price. Within adult society, the continued consequences of this are serious.

This seems criminal. Life is too short to be wasting possible opportunities for 'second-chance learning', especially when young people are in our schools for so many hours. Let's provide the framework for school to be 'done differently', on behalf of these vulnerable young people - so that they can do more than just attempt to survive. School can be a place of constancy and consistency for many who have experienced relational trauma and loss in their short lives to date. We all, as educational staff, can make a difference.

QUOTES FROM EDUCATION STAFF WHO WORK DIRECTLY WITH YOUNG PEOPLE WITH ATTACHMENT DIFFICULTIES

"A key adult can really make the difference".

"Use knowledge, understanding and compassion to stand firm. Keep breathing!"

"Behaviour is communication"

"It's never too late!"

"Stability is key"

"Have hope for these young people. Hope is contagious!"

"Be transparent & explicit"

"Stick with it".

"Raise the profile of the young person in a constructive way".

"Provide training for all staff that have contact with the young person – even the librarian!"

"Smile, say hello and use their name. Our interactions are so, so important."

"Have clear, consistent boundaries throughout".

"Flexibility of approach is a must!"

"Delve more into kids' backgrounds before making pronouncements"

"Be creative in your communication. Don't be restricted to a table or desk!"

'Remember they are watching and will notice so much more than we will ever realise'

'Young people with attachment difficulties have feelings too'

"If we pay attention to beginnings and endings, our schools will be better places for everyone."

In summary

- Preparation for the young person with attachment difficulties moving into any secondary provision is essential. This is not an optional extra

- A 'secure base' (a physical space) needs to be established in secondary provision that can be accessed regularly by the young person

- A key adult needs to be allocated to a young person with attachment difficulties. This relationship needs nurturing

- Check-ins are considered crucial for those with attachment difficulties and need to be encouraged, not frowned upon

- Education staff need to meet regularly to discuss and reflect upon these young people as a preventative course of action. Be wary of only being crisis-driven

- Make the most of any opportunities for fun, warmth and humour in your interactions with these young people

- We need to facilitate secondary schools to be reflective containers, not reactionaries (TACs)

- Home/school partnerships need to be maintained throughout secondary provision for these vulnerable young people

(continues ...)

- A minimum number of staff should be involved in any difficulties with young people

- Nominate a member of senior management to take the lead in any disciplinary action, rather than leaving that responsibility to whoever turns up first on the scene

- The key adult needs to be present and involved in any crises for translation, advocacy and follow-up work

- Integrate advice from different services/agencies into one support programme through the key adult

- Work towards less movement between different spaces and education staff within a young person's timetable

- Make the most of all of the emotional and social opportunities in school to make a difference in the young person's life

- If a young person has to leave - for whatever reason - do everything you can to give them a positive send-off with the opportunity for some sense of meaning and goodbyes

References

Bebbington, E. (2005) *'Stop Wasting My Time!' Case studies of pupil with attachment issues in schools with special reference to looked after and adopted children* Scotland: PAC

Bombèr, L.M. (2007) *Inside I'm Hurting: Practical strategies for supporting children with attachment difficulties in schools* London: Worth Publishing

Bowlby, J. (1969) *Attachment* (Volume I of Attachment and Loss) London: Hogarth Press

Bowlby, J. (1973) *Attachment and Loss Vol II: Separation* London: Hogarth Press

Cairns, K. (2004) *Learn the Child* London: BAAF

Cooper, G. et al (2000) Circle Of Security - Early Intervention Program For Parents And Children. www.circleofsecurity.org

Core 103: The Effects Of Abuse And Neglect In Child Development. (p.6&7) *The Pennsylvania Child Welfare Training Program.* www.pacwcbt.pitt.edu/Curriculum/Core%20103/

DfES (2003) *Managing Pupil Mobility: Guidance 0780* Nottingham: DfES

Geddes, H. (2006) *Attachment in the Classroom: The links between children's early experience, emotional well-being and performance in school* London: Worth Publishing

Golding, K.S., Dent, H.R., Nissim, R. & Stott, L. (2006) *Thinking Psychologically About Children Who Are Looked After and Adopted* Chichester: John Wiley &Sons

Golding, K. (2008) *Nurturing Attachments: Supporting children who are fostered or adopted* London: Jessica Kingsley Publishers.

Greenlagh, P. (1994) *Emotional Growth and Learning* New York: Routledge

Hughes, D.A. (1997) *Facilitating Developmental Attachment: The road to emotional recovery and behavioural change in foster and adopted children* Northvale, New Jersey: Jason Aronson Inc.

Kelly, A. (1997) *Talkabout - A Social Communication Skills Package* Milton Keynes: Speechmark Publishing

Kelly, A. (2004) *Talkabout - Building Self Esteem and Relationship Skills* Milton Keynes: Speechmark Publishing

Kelly, A. (2003) *Talkabout - Developing Social Communication Skills*
Milton Keynes: Speechmark Publishing

Morgan, N. (2007) *Blame My Brain!* London: Walker Books Ltd

National Children's Bureau (2007) *Understanding Why: Understanding attachment and how this can affect education* London: NCB

OCRD (Office of the Children's Rights Director) (2007) *Education Of Children In Care - About Education.* www.rights4me.org

Ofsted 070172 (2008) *Looked After Children - Good Practice In Schools.* www.ofsted.gov.uk

Ofsted 080181 (2008) *Future Care. Children's Advice On Future Care Standards. A Report by the Children's Rights Director For England.* www.rights4me.org

Ofsted 070139 (2008) *Children's Views On Advocacy: A Report By The Children's Rights Director For England.* www.rights4me.org

Scottish Executive (2008) *Count Us In - Improving The Education of our Looked After Children*

Social Exclusion Unit (2003) *A Better Education For Children In Care.* UK: socialexclusion.gov.uk

Sunderland, M. (2006) *The Science of Parenting* London: Dorling Kindersley

Winnicott, D.W. (1964) *The Child, The Family And The Outside World*
Harmondsworth: Penguin Group

How teachers can use a knowledge of attachment theory to work with difficult-to-reach teenagers

Marie Delaney

It is Friday afternoon in a secondary school. Year 10B1 are about to have their fourth lesson of the day - History. The teacher, Ms Baker, is considered a good teacher, with interesting approaches and excellent behaviour management strategies. 10B1 are considered a class of 'difficult' fifteen year olds. They are of mixed ability, and are, in theory, studying for GCSE History. Most of them have not chosen the subject for positive reasons. It was, in their opinion, the lesser of two evils in their options choices. Some did choose it because they enjoyed History in earlier years, but do they do not like the more formal format of the GCSE course.

Although some of the class are quite motivated and generally prepared to focus on their learning, a few pupils in this class have a reputation as being 'unteachable' and most teachers do not look forward to teaching them. Walking in, Ms Baker is met by the usual sight of some young people leaning back in chairs, laughing and joking; others are blatantly crouched over their mobile phones, checking their messages on Bebo. A group of girls is sitting at one table chatting. A couple of pupils who are sitting quietly at the front look up expectantly when Ms Baker enters, but most of the others ignore her entrance completely. One girl jumps up, wanting to talk privately, offering to help Ms Baker with her papers, asking if she can write the date on the board, arguing with another girl who is also trying to get the teacher's attention. Ms Baker wonders, as she often does, how she will get through the lesson, never mind teach them anything,

This scene, and variations of it, are played out in classrooms up and down the country every day. From my own experience as a secondary teacher of such classes and as an educational psychotherapist working with young people, I have become interested in what is happening in the teaching and learning process for those pupils who are considered almost 'unteachable'. In particular, I am interested in how an understanding of ideas from the therapy world, such as attachment theory, can help us, as teachers, to feel more resourceful when dealing with these young people in our classroom.

Who are these 'unteachables' ?

If we look at the example of Ms Baker's class, who might be in it? Let's look at some of the pupils more closely.

Alan

Alan is the boy sitting on his own, slouching, staring out of the window, headphones in his ears, apparently paying no attention at all to what is going on around him. He does not look up when Ms Baker enters and seems pre-occupied, 'in a world of his own'. When she attempts to gain the attention of the class and start the lesson, he turns up his music and starts to trace his name in the condensation on the window pane. Eventually, after his name has been called out three times for the register, he glances over and nods his head, before resuming his tracing on the window. The two boys sitting nearest him start prodding him in the back, laughing and asking what he is listening to on his iPod. Ms Baker can feel herself getting annoyed by this apparent disrespect and total lack of interest in her lesson.

PAUSE FOR THOUGHT

What is your immediate reaction to this situation?

What could be going on for Alan in this lesson?

What would you do as the teacher? Try to engage him or leave him alone?

Megan

Megan is sitting playing with her hair and chatting with some other girls. She comes up to the teacher's table as Ms Baker comes in and says she needs to talk to her privately about something that happened at home. She is quite insistent and gets upset when Ms Baker does not seem to have time for her. Ms Baker has spent a lot of her free time in earnest discussions with Megan, and last week Megan gave her a letter in which she suggested she was depressed and suicidal. She has also recently shown Ms Baker signs of self-harm - cuts on her arms, which she says she is doing more often. Ms Baker has had a few sleepless nights, even though she knew she had followed the school's Child Protection procedures correctly on this matter. She really feels that she should back away from Megan and let someone more experienced deal with her. Megan seems to be feeling very let down and is becoming increasingly aggressive in her attempts to get Ms Baker's attention. In every lesson, she insists on giving out the books and becomes very upset if the job is given to another pupil.

PAUSE FOR THOUGHT

What is your immediate reaction?

What might be going on for Megan and why is she reacting in this way to Ms Baker?

Is Ms Baker right in distancing herself from Megan? What would you do ?

Jake

Jake is sitting in the middle of the room, a tall, confident boy, seeming to take up a lot of space in the room and commanding the attention of the class in a way that Ms Baker cannot. He is throwing comments back and forth to other pupils who are vying to sit next to him. He seems to be able to do this and watch the reaction of the teacher at the same time. Ms Baker thinks Jake is a very intelligent boy but always feels there is some kind of competition about who is in charge of the lesson. She can get Jake to focus on his work but it always seems to be on his terms. He will often start asking about some part of the curriculum that they are not doing at that particular moment and insists on having his questions answered. Ms Baker feels torn between acknowledging his effort and interest, and being annoyed that he will not allow her to dictate the order of the lesson.

She knows that other teachers are very annoyed by him and are constantly discussing him in the staffroom.

PAUSE FOR THOUGHT

What is your immediate reaction to Jake?

What might be happening with him? Would you find Jake's behaviour annoying?

How would you react to his apparent need to control the lesson?

Sharon

Sharon comes into the class late. As usual she has not covered up her nose-ring, even though she knows this will result in her being sent to the Head. She refuses to sit in the only available chair and immediately starts hurling abuse at another girl in the class, a girl who last week seemed to be her best friend. She takes no notice of Ms Baker's attempts to calm her down. Ms Baker is confused because the previous week Sharon had been accompanied by a Behaviour Mentor, who had been very helpful in getting Sharon to settle and do her work. Today this person is not with her and Sharon will not work with her replacement. She is getting louder and louder and shouting that she hates Mrs Brown (the mentor), that she is too old and stupid and she will never have her in class with her again. After about five very disruptive (and very long) minutes, she flounces out of the room, saying she hates the class and Ms Baker is a rubbish teacher. She then continues to run up and down the corridor outside, banging on the doors of other classrooms, calling her friends on their mobile phones and refusing to come back when called by her new mentor.

PAUSE FOR THOUGHT

What is your immediate reaction to Sharon?

What is happening with her? What could you do as the teacher?

What would be your reaction to Sharon's rejection of her mentor?

Ms Baker

And what about the teacher, Ms Baker? How does she react and how does she feel? On this particular day Ms Baker says:

"I feel pretty defeated at the moment. I have worked so hard with some of these students and I think in general my behaviour management is good. I try to develop positive relationships with all my students. But really I sometimes wonder why they are in our school or why I am bothering!"

Ms Baker knows that there are days when her own mood and stress levels affect her teaching. She works hard to manage her own mental and physical state so that she has a positive frame of mind about this class. She knows that this is a key factor in being successful with difficult students. However, the scenario above took place on a day which had been going very well. She had been feeling good and was quite rested. She would have understood it if it had been a bad day for her. She knows that sometimes, when she is tired or stressed by other factors, she finds this class hard to deal with. However, it is surprising and depressing for her that she had so much trouble with them on a day when she was in a good mental and physical state. It is making her doubt the strategies which she had used to get into that positive and relaxed frame of mind.

What is happening with these young people?

We know that for most young people, good behaviour management strategies work most of the time. In general, being consistent, being fair, trying to build positive relationships, sanctioning inappropriate behaviour and rewarding appropriate behaviour will create classrooms where young people can learn. This teacher seems to be doing all this, and yet she is struggling to reach some of the students. These adolescents fall into a group of pupils, seemingly 'unteachable', who obviously need something more. In order to think about what might work, we need to stop and consider, from an attachment perspective, what is going on for these young people, that is different to others in the class. What are the issues getting in the way of these young people being in a state of readiness to learn, and allowing themselves to be taught?

What do we need to be in a good state for learning?

Any description of a good learner tends to include the following characteristics:

- → feels safe and is willing to take risks
- → has good self-esteem
- → can seek help when needed without expecting criticism or ridicule

→ is able to concentrate and be in what Gardner calls 'the flow' (1983)

→ is able to manage frustration, anxiety and disappointment

→ has the capacity to bear not knowing

→ is optimistic and has a positive attitude to a problem

→ can wait for attention

Moreover, in order to learn, a pupil needs to feel safe enough to accept the powerlessness and frustration of not knowing something. Learning takes place at that point where we struggle to match what we know with what seems to be new and different. Those who experience their internal and external worlds as dangerous may not be able to take this risk. When we look in more detail at the lives of the young people described above, we will see that they have often not had the opportunity to experience situations in which to learn these skills. For many, the opposite has taken place. Each young person in the examples above has had early childhood experiences which are affecting their capacity to learn and think in the classroom situation. Their behaviour may reflect insecure patterns of attachment

Patterns of attachment

INSECURE/AVOIDANT ATTACHMENT

Alan

Ms Baker eventually gets the attention of most of the class. She begins with a fun team game to revise some of the concepts from the last lesson. Alan does not open his books and keeps looking out of the window. Ms Baker is flummoxed as last week, when the lesson began with a team quiz, Alan participated well in his group. Although he did not offer any answers in the whole class, he had helped his group fill in some answers on the task sheet. What is the difference today? Ms Baker tries to engage Alan by reminding of his success last week and telling him that she had been really pleased with his efforts last week. He looks at her blankly and shrugs. Others in the class get restless and say "Leave him alone, Miss, ask me".

It is very tempting to leave Alan alone, but the teacher feels she needs to engage him, develop a relationship with him. When the class are doing another task, she quietly asks him how things are going and if she can help him. He shrugs and says nothing. She finds herself getting really annoyed.

Later in the staffroom, she discusses it with another teacher who says "Don't bother, you won't get anywhere with him. He's too stubborn. He just wants to do it on his own terms". Overhearing this, a maths teacher, says, "Oh, I have no problem with him, he is the best in the class and is always doing extra work". The other two teachers frown and exchange a meaningful look. Ms Baker thinks "Oh no, it must be me, I'm just not teaching him right". The other teacher thinks "Huh, bet he doesn't, he just wants to look better than us". All three teachers are left feeling unsettled by the interaction.

So what could be going on with Alan?

If we look at this in attachment terms, Alan seems to be displaying some of the characteristics of a learner with an *insecure avoidant attachment pattern*. If we look at what is working for him, we can see that, for whatever reasons, Alan is able to focus on a task on his own or in a group where the task is the main focus. He is not interested or able to benefit from a relationship with the teacher.

The insecure/avoidant attachment pattern of behaviour in schools

Young people like Alan have learned that if you seek attachment, you will be rejected. Their early childhood response has been to avoid seeking attachment. They have experienced a caregiver who is not available physically or emotionally. In adolescence, this may lead them to reject adult help - a kind of *"I'll reject you before you reject me"* stance. As they expect rebuff and rejection, they will not engage in relationships with adults which could expose them to this kind of rejection again.

How do we see this in class?

In class these young people often -

Show apparent indifference to the teacher	Seem unable and unwilling to accept help, denying the need for support	Say they don't care and shrug	Take refuge in the same kind of task and very quickly give up with any kind of new or more open-ended task
Show limited use of communication and creative opportunities; these require taking a risk with learning, which they are not prepared to do	Seem unprepared to engage and discuss a problem	Rip up their work, saying it is rubbish, before a teacher can comment on it	Ignore the teacher and avoid eye-contact
Do not like the teacher to stand in close proximity	Want to do tasks autonomously, even when they do not know what to do	Seem to be excessively pre-occupied with gadgets such as mobile phones or iPods	Their work is often not to the standard they want. Teacher input would be needed to improve it. They cannot allow themselves to accept this

These students may also present as the quiet young person who does not say much but is noticeably underachieving. Girls in particular may tend to internalise their pain, leading eventually, often in adolescence, to self-harm.

Insecure avoidant attachment pattern and the Learning Triangle

In the Learning Triangle formed between pupil, teacher and task (Geddes 2006), the focus for these young people is pupil-task, and they reject the need for the pupil-teacher relationship.

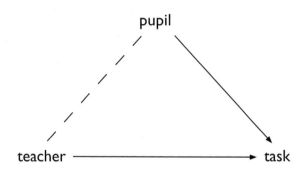

(Geddes 2006, p.77)

Despite their apparent indifference, these young people are also very anxious. They can put themselves under a lot of pressure by not wanting to admit they need help. They may be at risk of developing compulsive behaviours as they have a strong need to feel they have an element of control over their world.

Teaching strategies - what can we do about Alan?

So although we do not know much about Alan's background, if we choose to think about his learning and behaviour in attachment terms, it becomes important to understand what his underlying need is, what might be driving his behaviour. If his overwhelming desire is to show you, the teacher, that he does not need the relationship, we need to work with this; but equally, we need to help him to develop some trust in the relationship with us for any deeper learning to occur. If he insists on working on his own without help, there will come a point when he is not able to progress any further. However tempting, we will be colluding with his behaviour and not doing our job of teaching if we reject him further.

Often in schools, young people such as Alan refuse the help of a Teaching Assistant or teacher and seem very difficult to talk to, shutting down and not responding to well-meaning questions from people trying to help. They experience the relationship and questions as intrusive and dangerous. They can - as we saw in the above example with Ms Baker - provoke extreme annoyance in staff. We often feel that we really cannot 'teach' them or even discuss situations with them. We feel helpless. At this stage, the tendency, if we are not careful, is to ignore them or decide someone else needs to help them, not us. This is what I mean by colluding with the pattern of rejection.

What can the teacher do?

- ✓ Allow young people like Alan some control and choice over their activities where possible. This can often be built-in: for example, *"There are two practice tasks, you can choose to do them in the order you think is best"*

- ✓ Tasks are the key. Work through a task to develop a relationship around it. You can reach these young people by commenting on the task itself rather than trying to build a relationship directly. For example, you might say, *"That's an interesting idea. I was wondering how that girl felt when her friends all stopped texting her"* rather than saying *"I'm really pleased with the ideas you've come up with, how about adding how the girl felt?"* The second sentence has an in-built implication that you, the teacher, have some part to play! The first comment stays in the metaphor of the task, the story

- ✓ Try to find tasks these students enjoy doing, ones on which they can be fairly self-directed

- ✓ Organise group and project work - they will sometimes prefer to work with peers. However, as we have seen with Alan, the *type* of group task will still be important. If they can be involved, for example, writing answers on a worksheet, without having to interact too much with others, it will be easier for them

✔ Design tasks which involve a product rather than a process, for example making a booklet, designing a poster, writing a newspaper article. Avoidant young people like to see achievable goals. They can share their product without having to engage too much in the relationship

✔ The use of metaphor and story can be very successful with these students. Activities where they can draw, write or listen to stories, explore and discuss themes in books, on TV and film, use drama, objects and so on, will be safer than those which ask them to speak directly about themselves

✔ Left-brain, concrete, mechanical tasks - such as sorting, organising, categorising, building, clearing up - are all ways they can be involved in the daily routine of the class. They can help the class and teacher with a task such a wiping the board without acknowledging that they are doing it to improve their relationship!

✔ Work with other staff to ensure a consistent, positive approach which does not result in further rejection of the young person

What worked with Alan?

In Alan's case, it became very important to notice what type of tasks engaged him. He was able to take part in the group exercise when quiz questions were written, as the task was less verbally interactive. He also enjoyed work with a product, such as designing a newspaper story about the historical event being discussed. He enjoyed activities where he could correct his own work or could monitor that of another group, and where Ms Baker was able to build in elements of self-marking and peer marking into her lessons in preparation for the exams. He particularly liked keeping the score in group competitive activities. He was also motivated to do work on computers and was able to work with other students around this. By giving Alan clear tasks such as these, the Ms Baker was able to work on his peer and teacher relationships through the task.

It was also interesting to note that Alan enjoyed mathematics. The actual content of the curriculum can have unconscious meaning for some pupils. Mathematics can be a strange subject for some, as it involves thinking about whole things, parts of wholes, adding up, taking away and in general accepting the idea that splitting something into parts is safe. For those pupils with fragmented, complex, confusing relationships, there can be an unconscious resistance to these ideas. However, for some pupils, mathematics can become a refuge, as there are clear right and wrong answers. There is a structure and a process which lead you to a clear answer. The world seems clear and unambiguous. This may be its attraction to Alan. He can get lost in the task and come up with a satisfying, clear answer, with minimal input from the adult.

It is also worth noting, that Ms Baker had been trying to motivate Alan by saying how pleased she had been by his work in the previous lesson. For a learner such as Alan, the way to motivation may be by a slight change of emphasis in the praise. She could remind him how pleased he had been by his work last lesson. This allows him to be locus of control: his sense of pleasure-in-achievement is not dependent on his relationship with her.

Maintaining a consistent staff approach

The other teachers' reactions to this student show how important it is to work together to understand these young people. We can see in this example that it was easy for staff to feel that they are in opposing camps over Alan. This is not uncommon. It can be seen as an example of the psychological defence mechanism known as *splitting*, a way of dealing with the anxiety of not knowing how to deal with such pupils by taking up polarised positions. We need to be able to acknowledge this, notice when it is happening between ourselves and our colleagues, and be prepared to discuss our own feelings around the difficulties of working with pupils with whom we are not having success.

Jake

Jake seems to control the class, and is obviously 'the man' amongst his peers. He is of high ability and seems to want to continually challenge the teachers. If they suggest doing it one way, he will suggest another 'better' way. He asks questions as they occur to him, regardless of whether they are fitting in with the topic or where the rest of the class are. The other students seem to revere and fear Jake at the same time.

His family has quite a reputation in the area. His older brothers are in prison and his father was a well-known drug dealer who was shot. The incident made national news. His mother became very depressed after this and seemed to stop parenting her youngest child - Jake. She never comes to school events or to watch him perform in school musicals - he is a talented singer and actor. He has been suspended several times for arguing with teachers and fighting. Teachers in the staffroom think he is a menace, should be permanently excluded and that he wants things on his own terms all the time.

The Economics teacher, Ms Nash is surprised at this description as she finds him intelligent, hard-working and an independent learner. She has given him extra work at a higher level and he has been discussing doing Economics at university with her. She admires his independent spirit and the fact that he asks interesting, different questions. She is quite happy to let him draw up his own plan of work as long as he keeps to it. She is new to the school and does not come from the area, so she is unaware of the family reputation and did not teach any of his brothers.

What is happening with Jake?

Jake has learned from an early age that he cannot rely on adults for the care and nurturing he needs. His reaction, similar to Alan's, has been to decide that he does not need care or help and can manage by himself, and thus we can also think of him as showing an avoidant attachment pattern. Unlike Alan, who has unconsciously retreated from the relationship and learning, Jake's defence mechanism in psychological terms appears to be *omnipotence*, a need to control everything and everyone around him. This is particularly evident in the learning situations, as perhaps this is one of the few things he feels he can control in his life.

What worked with Jake?

Jake does not seem to react to praise as a motivator. Why should he? He has had no experience of this. His reference is internal and not external. Like Alan, he is motivated by language such as *"You know you can do this"*, rather than *"I know you can do this"*.

At the same time, he needs to experience a secure base, a sense of someone understanding him and giving a name to some of his emotions. It is likely the Economics teacher is doing this without realising it.

The strategies described above for working with Alan would all be useful for Jake. Unfortunately, we may often get into a battle for control with this 'type' of adolescent, and we can lose sight of their needs. Jake is actually a vulnerable young person, even though he might appear to be arrogant and dismissive of help.

Ms Baker agreed some targets for the month with Jake and allowed him some choice in the way he approached the tasks. She also arranged for him to have the necessary revision and practice books to work on outside school. She recognised that this was needed in order to let Jake feel in control of his learning. She let him know when she was available in her room after school if he needed to ask extra questions and asked him not to bring up these additional questions in the middle of the lesson, but to note them down to ask later.

Jake then appeared to settle down in Ms Baker's lesson and not disrupt the flow so often. Ms Baker was able to understand that Jake's attempts to be omnipotent actually stemmed from anxiety and fear of being unsafe, not from trying to challenge authority.

INSECURE AMIBIVALENT/RESISTANT ATTACHMENT

Megan

Megan is driving Ms Baker to distraction. Unlike Alan, she cannot focus on any task as she is constantly trying to get Ms Baker's attention. She gets upset at the start of the class because Ms Baker does not immediately acknowledge her attempts to help. Ms Baker knows that Megan likes to be acknowledged personally and to sit near her so that she can feel she is getting attention. Ms Baker takes care to greet Megan personally and comment on her new hairstyle. Having given her instructions, Ms Baker makes sure to come over and check that Megan knows what to do. Megan begins to say that she urgently needs to see her at break about "something very personal". Ms Baker is called over by another student who is having problems understanding the task. Megan watches her go, then starts calling loudly, "Miss, Miss, I don't know what to do. Can you come and help me?" Ms Baker says she will come back in a minute. Megan is quiet for a moment and then starts talking loudly to the girl next to her, saying that Ms Baker "is a stupid cow who can't explain anything properly".

Ms Baker snaps and says "Oh for heaven's sake, Megan, just learn to be patient and wait your turn". Megan sulks for the rest of the lesson, doing no work and disrupting the girls sitting near her with comments and jokes about the teacher.

Afterwards, when Ms Baker has taken refuge for her lunch, another teacher comes to tell her that Megan is outside and needs to speak to her urgently. Ms Baker feels guilty about her earlier impatience and leaves her lunch to go and talk to Megan. However, she feels resentful about this intrusion on her time.

What is happening for Megan?

Megan appears to be exhibiting an insecure/ambivalent-resistant attachment pattern of behaviour. She cannot focus on the task because she is too worried about maintaining the relationship with teachers. Megan's mother was suffering from alcohol addiction when Megan was born. She made several attempts to give up drinking and at times was able to parent Megan in a safe way. When drinking, her moods could become violent or tearful and she was unable to cope with Megan's infant demands. Megan has learned that you cannot trust the mood of adults and that you need to be hyper-vigilant in monitoring the relationship you have with them. She cannot believe that when an adult leaves you, they can still think about you and 'hold you in mind'. She has not had any experience of this. She therefore needs to stay close to the teachers, perceives other young people as competing for the scarce resource of the teacher's attention and cannot take her attention away from the relationship for long enough to do the task.

The insecure and ambivalent/resistant pattern
of behaviour in schools

As we can see with Megan, these children cannot predict their mother's response and so are reluctant to leave her side. An infant who has been rebuffed, not picked up or attended to when seeking consolation, will often increase his or her attempts to get a response. The child might become clingy, constantly seeking reassurance that he is cared for. There were times when the caregiver was emotionally and physically available and other times when she was not. The child's attempts to connect with an adult are fuelled by anxiety and a need to check out the relationship. In school, young people with this kind of background may sometimes continue to seem more helpless than they really are, because they want to keep the connection with a key adult. This is particularly problematic at adolescence because staff often expect students to be independent, to be able to work on their own and do not expect to have to constantly reassure them that they are being kept in mind.

How do we see this in class ?

In school these adolescents are often -

Those who find it hard to maintain suitable boundaries with staff, often wanting to exchange very personal information	Those adolescents who, even when old enough, refuse to go out at break times because they want to stay close to the teacher at all times	Unable to focus on the task in case they lose the attention of the teacher	Feel very rejected if the teacher does not return their confidences or passes them on to another member of staff
Able to use spoken language very skilfully in order to maintain the teacher's attention	Overly dependent on the teacher	In need of constant reassurance	Quick to become abusive and rude if they feel they are being ignored
Labelled manipulative	Trying to get very close to a particular teacher, and wanting to tell them all their problems	Unable to take independent action	Very anxious

Insecure ambivalent attachment pattern
and the Learning Triangle

In the Learning Triangle (Geddes 2006, p.97), the student's focus is on the teacher-student relationship to the detriment of the student-task aspect of the triangle.

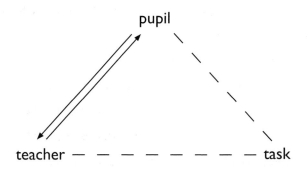

(Geddes 2006, p.97)

In learning terms, these adolescents often underachieve, especially with literacy, as they are too busy paying attention to maintaining the relationship verbally and cannot focus on a task. For them the task is dangerous, as it involves separation and leaving the adult. As they have often had little experience of being thought about, they cannot believe that the relationship with the adult will continue when they are not in close proximity or in the room with them.

As Ms Baker has discovered, this type of student can be very wearing on the teacher's patience and emotional energy as they are continually working to get the teacher's attention. It does not seem to matter how much positive attention they get, it never seems enough for them. Indeed, they may seem blaming and resentful, holding grudges and saying that the teacher is not fair to them, even when they have had an inordinate amount of extra attention. Unfortunately, their behaviour gets described as 'immature', 'attention-seeking' and 'manipulative', and teachers may become impatient and react angrily. They can become isolated from their peers, who are irritated by their continual need for adult attention and their apparent persecution complexes.

Teaching strategies - what can we do about Megan?

The temptation with these young people is to give them what they demand. Often a Teaching Assistant is appointed to sit with them to ensure they get on with their work. If we are not careful, an adolescent with this pattern of insecure attachment behaviour can unconsciously make use of the situation so that the helper does a lot of the work for them. They may end up constantly nagging the student to get on with the task, staying with them to make sure they keep on track. In the long-term, this is not helping the young person develop the required separation for learning to take place. These students may seem as if they cannot learn. It is important not to collude with their behaviour, but to take an empathic, boundaried stance and recognise the anxiety that is driving how they behave.

Strategies which might help therefore are those which reassure that the student can be held in mind whilst at the same time encouraging them to make small steps to independence. For example,

- ✔ Set small timed tasks, using ways for the student to mark the time - making sure they can check on a watch or phone
- ✔ Gradually increasing the duration of these tasks
- ✔ Let the young person know that you will get back to them, and when that will be. You might say, for example, *"Try the first three questions on your own and then I will come back and check"*.
- ✔ Make sure you do come back, and that if you get distracted, you acknowledge what has happened: *"I am sorry I did not get back to you when we agreed, that must have been worrying for you. You probably thought I had forgotten you but I had not"*. It is not necessary to be a 'perfect' teacher, keeping to your time frames exactly, but it is important to acknowledge the anxious feelings it can arouse in these students.
- ✔ Avoid the temptation to over-help. These young people need to experience some frustration in order to develop their ability to problem-solve and learn. You can acknowledge how frustrating learning like this

can be. *"I know it feels impossible to do without the teacher next to you. It can feel very frustrating when we are learning something new. You can trust your brain to do it though".* Over-helping can actually be very unhelpful, leading these students to continue to rely on behaviour which can seem manipulative, but which perhaps, up to now, has been their only way of getting their needs met.

What worked with Megan

Ms Baker worked hard to understand her feelings about Megan. She realised that she was feeling manipulated into giving Megan a lot of attention which did not improve her approach to work. She tried to reassure Megan in class that she would come back to check in with her at regular intervals. She stopped coming out from the staffroom on demand at lunchtime, and set aside a fifteen minute slot on two days a week when Megan could come to see her. She also assigned an older peer mentor to keep an eye on Megan at break-times and encourage her to join in activities. She realised that she could be the first point of contact, but that she needed to help Megan to separate from her and know she could be still thought about.

INSECURE DISORGANISED ATTACHMENT

Sharon

Ms Baker has no idea how anyone can teach Sharon. Sharon has hardly ever stayed in her lesson and Ms Baker often sees her running around the school building. Some members of staff have told her not to worry about it, as "that girl should not be here anyway", but somehow Ms Baker feels this is not good enough. She has noticed that the learning support unit staff and head of year are having a meeting about Sharon. She wonders if she would be allowed to attend.

What is happening with Sharon?

Sharon does not appear able to develop relationships with staff or peers. She is also unable to focus on the task. Sharon comes from a fragmented, complex family, where there has been a history of abuse and neglect. She was taken into care when she was five and has had numerous foster placements in the last ten years. Her placements usually break down a result of her seemingly uncontrollable behaviour, or when her mother is granted custody for short periods. Three other brothers and two sisters are living with their birth father. Sharon has been told that her father did not want to take her and her mother had been forced to keep her against her will. There are many services trying to engage with the family, with varying degrees of success.

Sharon would seem to be exhibiting behaviour very typical of an insecure disorganised attachment pattern. She seems unable to benefit from either the relationship or the task aspect of learning.

The insecure/disorganised attachment pattern
of behaviour in schools

Young people like Sharon often come from chaotic, damaged backgrounds, and have usually suffered severe neglect, violence and/or abuse. They seem erratic in their responses and can display very distressing behaviours which put them or others at risk. It is not always possible to see the immediate trigger to their extreme behaviour. They are very difficult to teach and the most challenging to respond to, but fortunately they constitute the smallest percentage of pupils in the insecure attachment group.

How do we see this in class?

Their erratic responses and distressing behaviours make it very difficult to maintain these adolescents in a classroom situation.

They often -

Become very abusive to the other children in the class	Get very frustrated and show this by banging their heads against the wall	Run around uncontrollably or run out of class unexpectedly	Explode into temper for no apparent reason
Change from being very agitated to 'switched off'. They might be loudly demanding your attention one minute and the next, telling you they do not need you and to go away	Can be very abusive to the teacher, rubbishing their attempts to teach	Truant classes and bully other students into coming with them	Become very aggressive with their peers, making other students wary of them and unwilling to spend time with them

It is difficult to plan for these students, as they may respond differently from week to week. They expect the worse - which indeed, has usually happened already - and cannot believe that anyone would consistently care about them. They are, in fact, focused on survival. They have a constant need to be hyper-vigilant, looking out for dangers, real and imagined. It can help if we remember that much of their difficult behaviour is prompted by fear and overwhelming anxiety. They quite simply have no space in their minds to think or engage in relationships or learning.

Insecure disorganised attachment pattern and the Learning Triangle

These young people are not engaged with either relationship or task within the Learning Triangle. I often feel that they are floating above it or around it. These are the adolescents we will feel most helpless about. We need to be careful that our own feelings of helplessness do not turn into punitive approaches. We can find ourselves reacting angrily to their destructive behaviour because we feel completely useless in our attempts to help.

Teaching strategies - what can we do about Sharon?

The key task in working with these students is to acknowledge the strain put on us by their chaotic behaviour. Their erratic behaviour and unpredictable responses can mean that we become very anxious ourselves when working with them. Unexpected eruptions, aggression, persistent refusal to co-operate or focus on the lesson, and an apparent lack of respect or empathy towards others are wearying experiences on a daily basis, and attack the thinking capacity of the teacher. We need to see our task as maintaining and restoring our own capacity to think, and, subsequently, the student's. Some ideas which might help are to:

- ✔ Have a strong peer and outside support group for yourself. Other professionals, such as educational psychologists, social workers and counsellors can be useful to talk with and discuss what is going on
- ✔ Have a clearly marked routine and structure to your classes. These adolescents cannot cope with sudden change and need to know there is a structure, even if they appear to kick against it
- ✔ Use visual timetables if appropriate to show the daily routines. Remember and cater for the fact that emotionally, these adolescents are far younger than their chronological age
- ✔ Flag up any changes to routine in advance if possible, and reflect back how catastrophic a change might feel to such a young person. Say for example, *"I know changes can feel terrible and you feel as if you cannot bear someone going away, but we will be able to manage it OK"*.
- ✔ If there are going to be many changes in the day, for example involving supply teachers, think about allowing this student to work somewhere

    safe with a trusted adult

✔   If that is not possible, have a back-up plan if they erupt in class, or give them a time-out card to use

✔   Transitions and endings need to be carefully planned and acknowledged (*and see* Chapter 2). The idea, for example, that you do not tell your class you are leaving until the last possible minute is a disaster with adolescents with a history of disorganised attachment. They need to experience an ending which is planned, allows them to have feelings of grief, to be supported to reflect on these feelings, and survive

What worked with Sharon?

For Sharon, the school building, and in particular the learning support unit, became a secure base for her. Sharon needed her overwhelming negative feelings 'contained' by the adults around her, but in the first instance, it was the building itself which provided this containment. It came to represent a secure physical base for her. It was a place where

→   rules and boundaries were clear

→   routines were established

→   in general, the day was predictable

→   the roles of adult and adolescent were clear

The adults in this situation had to work hard not to blame each other and to maintain their own thinking around Sharon.

Developing a plan for all staff who work with Sharon

Although the mentors who were trying to work with Sharon felt quite despondent, they recognised that she came to school every day looking for answers to her problems, and they believed that school was still her best

chance. They decided to have a case study meeting to try to understand her needs from the attachment perspective. Ms Baker attended this meeting, as she thought it might help her in her dealings with Sharon.

The group started by looking at what was known about Sharon's history. It was particularly important for them to look at times when things had been working with Sharon, and to understand what might have been unhelpful on the occasions when things had gone wrong. They realised that Sharon had not been able to trust the success of her relationship with the behaviour mentor, and had rejected it.

Hard as this was to understand, the mentors reflected in their meeting on what had happened so that they might continue to work with Sharon.

What experience had Sharon ever had of this type of personal interest and positive attention? Her early childhood was marked by abusive relationships and domestic violence. She had little experience of developing a trusting relationship with an adult. Perhaps this is why she had to sabotage it - it felt too dangerous to allow someone close. It was precisely because the mentor was getting through her barriers, that she had, at some level, to reject her. Moreover, Sharon quite literally did not have space in her brain to think about learning: her internal anxieties did not allow this.

They also discussed why the principle of normal 'behaviour management' might not work with Sharon. Behaviour management strategies are based on a series of assumptions, which may not be valid for students like her.

ASSUMPTION I POSITIVE ATTENTION LEADS TO BETTER BEHAVIOUR

Many behaviour management theories work on the assumption that rewarding appropriate behaviour and sanctioning inappropriate behaviour will lead young people to learn better behaviour. This is how the behaviour mentor had been trying to work with Sharon. But in the discussion, she realised that life had taught Sharon a different lesson - that positive attention (a reward) cannot be trusted. Strange as it might seem, Sharon was only comfortable with negative feedback, as this was what she was used to.

ASSUMPTION 2   CHOICE IS A GOOD THING

Many of the strategies being used with Sharon relied on the idea that choice is a good thing, that if we give a child responsibility and discuss rights and consequences, they will behave better and be able to learn. Again, the life circumstances of young people like Sharon have taught them differently. They have learnt that they have no control over their own or their family's circumstances. They cannot perceive themselves as individuals who can make a choice, even a simple one, and certainly not over important issues. They have rarely had experience of an adult asking their opinion or taking their wishes into account. When faced with having to make a choice, perhaps especially one about behaviour, they can react in different ways - become compliant and passive, or aggressive and argue: act in or act out.

ASSUMPTION 3   THE STUDENT'S STAGE OF DEVELOPMENT
MATCHES THEIR AGE

We tend to assume that young people have reached certain emotional and social developmental stages which relate to their chronological age. Secondary schools in particular are set up on the assumption that young people have negotiated certain life stages successfully. There is an inherent assumption, for example, that they

- can take turns in a group
- can show a teacher that they are listening without interrupting with their own stories
- can wait for attention
- are able to accept help and do not expect ridicule for needing it

- can explain their wants and needs in a socially acceptable way
- are able to manage and express their emotions in an acceptable way most of the time
- have a respect for other people's personal space

Sharon had not progressed through some of these stages. She had some of the coping behaviours of a toddler. She expected ridicule, denigration and catastrophe in every situation. She had not had the secure start to allow her to develop and learn these skills.*

The way targets had been set for Sharon

The group considered why some of Sharon's targets were so difficult to meet. They realised she had no reference experience for them, that she had never had an experience of doing such things nor of an adult naming the experience for her.

For example, Sharon had been set the target of sitting still and showing that she could concentrate on her own work for ten minutes. This assumed that she had a way of knowing when this was happening. How does a child know what it is like to be concentrating, what lets them know that they are doing this thing called 'focusing'? If they have had very few experiences of this, either from a shared experience with a thinking adult or on their own in a calm environment, how can they understand what we are asking for and how will they know if they are doing it?

Knowing about something in theory, and experiencing it in person, are two different things. At some stage in our life, someone needs to put a name to these

For more on why behaviour management strategies are unlikely to work with children and young people with attachment difficulties, please see Teaching the Unteachable, Delaney, 2008, Worth Publishing, pp.31-44)

experiences so that we know what they are. As young people, we need adults to help us make sense of our experience and name the experiences we are having. Sharon had not had this opportunity.

What was planned?

The mentors were able to devise activities in the learning support unit which worked on letting Sharon experience some of the skills she had not developed. As Sharon had not learnt appropriate social skills at an earlier age, they chose games which were designed for a younger child but which an adolescent would still enjoy playing. For example, Sharon often wanted to play games with other pupils but would inevitably spoil them by cheating. The mentors began to incorporate card games and competitive games into the curriculum so that she could fulfill her aggressive desires in a safe way. They could then comment on the difficulty of allowing other people to win or know more. They were careful not to comment directly on what was happening, but to use more general language such as -

"It can feel very difficult to lose or to let other people have a go. Some people feel this is like letting them take over everything".

In a special circle time they played games which allowed Sharon to experience the feeling of concentrating, for example, 'Wink Murder'. At the end of each game, they asked the class to name each skill practised and to notice when they were doing it. They built on Sharon's love of drama and involved her in small role-plays, where she could practise being the teacher and playing out her anger and anxiety.

They agreed to have weekly review meetings and to give Sharon a weekly certificate which stated three successes in the skills worked on and one thing to work on for next week. Whenever Sharon tore a certificate up, they said "Sometimes it can be very difficult to hear good things about ourselves and to believe they are true". If Sharon was excluded, they made it clear that she was welcome back and that they would continue to work on the issues with her. In this way, Sharon moved forward in small steps, neither too large to scare her nor too small to leave her where she was.

What teachers can do

It is important that staff try to see beyond the seemingly impossible behaviour of students such as Sharon, to understand why a young person might have a *need* to control everything. It was important not to reject Sharon in the way that she was rejecting the staff.

Initially it will be other staff, such as the learning support unit team or learning mentors, who will need to spend time on some intensive work with pupils such as Sharon.

You may be thinking that some of the work described above is not possible in class. However, it is possible as a mainstream teacher to try to understand what the behaviour is showing you about the internal anxieties and fantasies which are getting in the way of learning.

By her attendance at meetings where staff tried to understand what was happening, Ms Baker was able to realise the problem was not about her 'bad' teaching skills. She said "It helped me to realise that my feelings are normal and that there is no easy answer for Sharon. I tried to keep to a routine in my class and to practise the technique of 'wondering aloud' about her feelings and behaviour. I made a point of saying hello to her, even if she was angry and upset. I tried some of the drama, games and drawing techniques suggested by the mentors. They sometimes worked and sometimes didn't, but I no longer took it so personally. I realised that school was the safest place for Sharon to act out and protest and that I needed to stick to my boundaries, even if she kicked hard against them".

What happened to Sharon?

Sharon managed to get through to year 10 in mainstream education. She was then placed on an alternative curriculum, including a one-day work placement, on which her mentor initially accompanied her. With some support, she did succeed in this placement and finished year 11. She might not have appeared in the school league tables, but Ms Baker and the staff involved with her felt some satisfaction at enabling her to get to a point where she could survive in the outside world.

Understanding behaviour as communication
- what can teachers do differently?

This is not a meant to be a story of a teacher's or young people's failures, but rather a discussion of what has been found to work. Although Ms Baker found this class difficult to teach, she was pro-active in her approach, and in all cases was prepared to try to understand what was going on for her pupils. She worked in a school which supported this ethos and where there were other staff also struggling to find a different perspective. Through thinking about these young people in a slightly different way, she realised that she had developed some new approaches in her teaching. These can be summarised as follows:

- ✔ Expand your ways of noticing what is going on
- ✔ Think consciously about what underlying defence mechanisms might be in operation. Recognise what comes from you and what comes from the child
- ✔ Practise thinking about the child in terms of attachment styles
- ✔ Practise using all your senses to notice what is happening
- ✔ Re-frame the young person's behaviour and ask what *need* it is showing you
- ✔ Practise breaking the expected pattern of response

✔ Pay attention to emotional health. For example, at the beginning of a class, have a quick check-in of how people are feeling

✔ Get precise and curious about language. Use it to:

  → be specific about social and emotional skills, recognise and acknowledge them in all situations, for example, *"Thanks for waiting patiently, I know that can be hard"*

  → create a positive expectation of these students, for example *"Ms Jones was telling me how well you did last lesson"*

  → motivate pupils according to their own attachment style, for example, *"You know you can do this"* or *"I know you can do this"*, as appropriate.

  → wonder aloud and provide commentaries for what might be happening internally, for example, *"I wonder if anyone is feeling a bit fed up with this as it is getting more complicated"*

✔ Develop real active listening skills which do not involve searching for solutions and suggestions. Take the time to listen to the whole communication

✔ Expand your planning skills to include planning tasks which take into account the student's attachment needs, as well as emotional and social development needs

✔ Remember to include left-brain tasks as differentiation for calming down if needed, in the same way that you include activities for early finishers

✔ Include games which allow young people to develop play skills

✔ Work with metaphor and creativity such as stories, drama, art

✔ Manage your own state for teaching. Develop conscious strategies to get into the right state and out of unproductive states

✔ Learn as much as you can about other people who can help

✔ Remember that parents/carers will have the same anxieties and issues around the behaviour of the child. Strive to understand this, and avoid a blaming approach

✔ Find people who are working well and learn from them. What do they believe about these young people? How do they act around them? How do they respond to critical incidents?

In summary

- In any secondary classroom, regardless of the skill of the teacher, there are adolescent pupils who seem unreachable and unteachable, who may have attachment difficulties

- 'Normal' behaviour management strategies are based on a set of assumptions which may not be valid for these pupils

- Early childhood experiences of loss, trauma and violence may have affected how these young people behave and their capacity to learn in class

- Teachers often come to represent key attachment figures in these students' lives

(continues ...)

- An understanding of attachment theory can help teachers think about these pupils in a different way. It can enable us to understand the underlying anxieties and needs being expressed through their challenging behaviour

- Noticing and framing behaviour in terms of attachment patterns, and as communication about needs, will lead to the development of different strategies for working with hard-to-teach adolescents

References

Delaney, M. (2009) *Teaching the Unteachable: Practical ideas to give teachers hope and help when behaviour management strategies fail* London: Worth Publishing.

Gardner, H. (1983) *Frames of Mind: The Theory of Multiple Intelligences* New York: Basic Books

Geddes, H. (2006) *Attachment in the Classroom: The links between children's early experience, emotional well-being and performance in school* London: Worth Publishing

Exterior fortresses and interior fortification

Use of creativity and empathy when
building an authentic attachment relationship in school

Barbara Earl

Teachers have always given a great deal of thought to meeting the needs of young people whose emotional and behavioural development has been impeded. For these pupils, the world of school can be a baffling place in which to function. Certain norms regarding behaviour and attitude are expected, norms which can represent exacting standards for those already feeling adrift in a sea of turbulent emotions.

The effects of problematic experiences in their early relationships contribute immensely to the teenager's distrust of the intentions of those in authority. Sadly, some young people can have very good reason to adopt such a guarded and inflexible view of the intentions of the adults around them. Unrecognised feelings of hurt, hate, anger and fear incubate a sense of grievance and alienation; disengagement from the ethos of the school and the demands of the wider community follows. Lethargy and faulty decision-making processes prevent the student from accessing the curriculum and benefitting from the varied opportunities for personal growth offered by the school. Unmet need fans the flames of rage and despair which deplete the young person's vitality and ability to select pro-social choices.

In response to the difficulties presented by the student, we usually initiate a range of support to try to help the individual adjust more effectively to the requirements of the curriculum, and to the need to relate well to others. Quite often, this support will be in the form of a patchwork cloak of interventions placed over the reality of the student's week. We direct a lot of time and effort, for example, at providing free-floating programmes of dyslexia tuition, 'anger-management' sessions and reading recovery. Whilst there is nothing intrinsically wrong with this sort of support, it may be viewed by the young person as an imposition rather than a help, if it stands alone as a kind of educational band-aid. In a similar way, we may set wide-ranging targets in the vain hope of closing the gap between the student and the aims of the school. As professional education staff, we can experience a great deal of frustration when these plans begin to falter, and be at a loss to explain why the overall scheme has had little or no beneficial effects.

To the student, the burden of being the focus of the unspoken disappointment of others is yet more evidence of the failure of those around her to understand and respond appropriately to her needs. Shame and resentment can lead to defiance. This can sometimes translate into staff seeing the young person as intractable and culpable for all of the difficulties being experienced by the key players. The general sense of failure can lead to a strengthening of the very defence mechanisms which our interventions sought to ameliorate. Our benign but misjudged efforts are no match for the inner fortification of the angry young person.

To begin to gently breach the student's defences, and allow the support to have any chance of being beneficial, we need to place an *authentic attachment relationship* at the heart of whatever plans we come up with. It is the presence of an empathic attachment figure, standing by the individual pupil and managing the raft of interventions, which will be the defining component of any enterprise seeking to bring about change for the young person.

However, the danger inherent in such a proposal is the possibility that those of us taking up this role may unwittingly adopt an authoritarian stance and try to force through a relationship in a heavy-handed manner which lacks a sense of mutual influence. By this I mean that the 'offer' of relationship may seem overbearing and coercive to the sensitive student. Time can feel short in schools; it is easy to be tempted to work at our own adult pace. Such potential over-intensity and haste may un-balance the fragile early stages of a pairing.

Unhelpful starts like this will fail to encourage feelings of trust and goodwill on the part of the young person who, not unnaturally, may resist the opportunity to be 'drenched in the syrup' of the adult's good intentions. The teenager is likely to react more positively to an approach which suggests that due regard will be paid to his dignity and independence.

Richard, a sixteen-year old pupil with behavioural difficulties was paired with a well-meaning but talkative key worker. He was confident enough to raise his negative feelings about the arrangement. Speaking in the direct and no-holds-barred manner of the disgruntled adolescent he explained that his key worker was, "Jarring, miss - she doesn't stop talking!"

By this, I took him to mean that he was reacting against feelings of being impinged upon and talked at in an inconsiderate way. Too many questions led to Richard having a sense of being interrogated rather than acknowledged with care and concern. Richard's programme was adjusted with immediate effect, and the member of staff was given some training on more effective communication.

Creative activity as buffer

It is my belief and experience that creative activity can be used as a safe way to introduce the adolescent student with attachment difficulties to working closely with a particular adult. The buffer provided by the piece of art-work allows the student and us to make a real connection with each other. In addition, it then becomes possible for us to identify and work at precisely the point at which the young person is operating.

A creative piece has the added advantage of allowing work to take place in companionable silence if needed. Non-verbal communication, such as warm eye contact, offers us a replacement for speech as a means of connecting with the student in a joint or complementary activity. Teenagers who are loath to converse can feel in touch with the adult without believing themselves to be trapped in an unwanted conversation. This element of simplicity permits the growth of genuine relationship, built upon trust, and tended with kindness and a light touch by the adult.

In this chapter I will discuss the importance of establishing this all-important attachment relationship with the troubled teenager. First, I will explore the usefulness of the role of the attachment figure in effecting change. I will then describe in detail my work with Tony, a teenager with deep emotional needs; a case study which I hope will illustrate both the importance of the creative activity and the core elements of this gentle approach. Further commentary on this method will follow with shorter vignettes, and finally, I will provide a summary of the main ideas and approaches.

Understanding the pivotal role of the attachment figure as agent of change will help those who work with troubled teenagers to reach them in a more fruitful way. Adolescents live in dread of being subjected to the seemingly endless whims and requirements of adults: as Dawn, aged fifteen, put it, *"I don't need another mother, I've got one of those at home!"*. The growth of a genuinely supportive relationship with one particular adult can lead eventually to willingness on the student's part to benefit from the wider plan of provision. Mutual respect and planned interventions provide a container for the young person's hidden dependency needs and, as a result, over time, fewer outbreaks of emotional distress will arise throughout the school day.

The role of the attachment figure in effecting change

The key-worker-as-attachment-figure must be the hub of any plans. The availability of this reliable and caring adult, to act as champion for the young person as he negotiates his way through the process of change, is essential. This colleague will be low on fault-finding and high on acceptance, thus providing a sound container for the student's anxieties and troubling emotions. For those taking this role, it will be our ability to welcome, listen actively and reflect upon moods and feeling states that will bring the relationship alive. Gerhardt (2004) writes that it is the power of *'a smile, a way of putting feelings and thoughts into words'* that will allow the individual to feel deeply understood and supported (p.214). Without this attachment figure at the centre of support strategies, the student will not fully access the programmes that are offered and may come to reject them, as described above.

The attachment team

In any Learning Support Team comprised of teachers, Higher Level Teaching and Learning Support Assistants, Inclusion Workers and Learning Mentors, there will be a variety of personalities, skills and preferred styles of delivery. When deciding to set up such a pivotal attachment-based relationship, it is important that the school SENCO[1] or Learning Support Manager considers the compatibility of key-worker and young person. The emotional maturity of team members will be the most significant element in the overall plan of provisions; other colleagues will be able to contribute towards the meeting of discrete learning needs or welfare issues.

What matters most is that the key-worker is enabled to meet the safety and acceptance needs of the student, whilst co-ordinating the range and delivery of the agreed support plan with sensitivity. The key-worker is the embodiment of the secure base offered by the school, and as such, is the lead figure in understanding that disruptive and perplexing behaviour is often an expression of the young person's desire for connection and genuine communication.

The young person can, of course, take a full part in discussions as to the most suitable choice of key worker. This involvement is essential if the student is to feel committed to the project in any real sense.

Beginning

There will be times when the Learning Support Manager will find that the creation of this alliance is straightforward. Certain individual pupils may immediately warm to the prospect of working closely with a particular member of staff, and accept the offer with alacrity. The old phrase, *"When the student is ready, a teacher will appear"*, holds true for some.

For the most vulnerable young people, however, such a relationship may need to be more formally arranged and stage-managed. Guntrip (1971) advises that we should guard against mentally invading those whom we seek to help, and that we need to respect the individual's fear of *'being helped against his will'* (p.189). Those who have not previously felt themselves to be well-supported may find it difficult to enter into such an arrangement, even if they have had some input into the selection of the adult. The entire enterprise may feel a rather daunting prospect, and too rich for the student to consider and accept if he or she has not been accustomed to the kind of intensity found in a one-to-one relationship. It is best to be mindful that some young people need to be able to control their proximity to others and may feel uncomfortable and threatened if this requirement is either ignored or, even worse, deliberately overlooked. Without the protective support of a larger group, the young person may reject the overwhelming prospect of an exclusive relationship. For these adolescents, the collaborative strength of the whole team is needed, which the student may view as less threatening (*and see below,* p.183, Chapter 7).

The therapeutic team

It may be advisable to deploy a 'therapeutic team' to work alongside the key-worker, especially when starting to work with those who display evidence of a disorganised attachment pattern (*see* p.85), for example, through extreme and chaotic behaviours. Reliable and consistent educational and emotional input can be offered alongside other students in a shared venue by a number of like-minded colleagues, in a co-ordinated way: for example, inviting the student to join a discrete project such as a girls' group exploring Sex and Relationship Education, or a mixed group undertaking a media project.

This kaleidoscope of support may be easier for the young person to accept. Too much emotional input can be as bad as too little, and a team working together will serve to diffuse anxiety and tension and, ultimately, strengthen the bond between the future key-worker and young person. As rapport grows it may become possible to focus upon underlying issues and more individualised support needs.

An invitation for an exploratory chat in a relaxed setting may be enough to persuade most adolescents with attachment difficulties to at least try to engage. Others may initially prefer to be part of an informal support group, becoming, for example, involved in lunchtime activities such as a games, DVD, or sports clubs.

Practical considerations

Whichever route we take, this kind of individual support will require regular sessions away from the classroom, at least initially. The approach, content and mode of delivery may well differ from a more formal classroom arrangement. In the beginning, I have found it helpful to offer six sessions to establish the importance of fixed meetings, with an option to extend if both student and key worker are in agreement.

There are also cost implications for the school, since experienced staff who have expertise with teenagers who present challenging behaviour can be expensive. In the long term, however, there are wide ranging advantages for the school community. The student around whom the support is centred will, of course, gain enormously from reliable contact with an adult who has the time to show a genuine interest in their emotional well-being and attainment. The teaching and learning of peers will suffer less interruption, owing to the positive effects of the intervention. Teachers and key workers benefit from working collaboratively in the development of effective communication techniques, differentiation and assessment for learning.

The light touch: working one-to-one with the troubled teenager

Govern a child as you would cook a very small fish   Chinese proverb

When working with young people who may have good reason to distrust the motives of those around them, I have found that it best to advance with tact and delicacy. The task-driven focus of much of school life can, at times, militate against the use of a subtle approach. The gifts of time and choice, however, are immensely powerful tools in the setting up of the supportive relationship. It is too often the soothing elements of time and attention that are missing from the life of the young person. It is helpful to formalise these essentials, and provide the young person with their own appointment card to keep in school both to remind them of key times and serve as a token of your support.

A short initial introductory session to discuss plans for intervention and to ascertain the parent's and the young person's thoughts can start the process of regular meetings. For those who seem reluctant to engage or too anxious or angry to relax, it can be best at the start of the second session to set out various activities in advance. It helps if these are not strictly curriculum-based in the first instance; a sand-tray, textile, game, jigsaw, collage or drawing materials will be most appropriate. As the young person arrives for the session, it can sometimes be productive for the adult to be found engaged in one of the activities. We can give a warm greeting to welcome the student, who will be pleasantly surprised at not being explicitly directed to a task by the omnipotent presence of the teacher. The young person may become inquisitive, will often ask about the work and generally opt to join in. If not, the activity can be set aside without undue fuss. More often than not, the young person will choose to engage, or suggest another activity, as this low-key way of negotiating the all-important beginning has felt acceptable to him. The session may then progress.

The activity forms a safe link between the adult and young person, who may feel relief that he is not being pressured into a discussion of his problems, characterised by the unveiling of the unvarnished truth! Informal discussion about how the week has progressed so far may take place, if appropriate, or teacher and student may simply enjoy the activity together as co-workers involved in a session of non-threatening response and exchange.

Geddes (2006) suggests that an appropriate and well-planned task can be a powerful emotional safety net for many students, reducing anxiety and acting as a conduit through which the pair may begin to communicate either verbally or non-verbally, or both. For some students with attachment difficulties, engaging with the task may symbolise the frightening challenge of relating to the demands of the outside world.

We must be prepared to go at the pace of the student, as this will allow him to feel that his boundaries and protective defences have been respected. The idea is that teacher and student work alongside each other in an unhurried, co-operative way. These practical, play-based sessions should be warm in tone and introduce elements of fun into the experience of relating. The sessions fulfil the student's requirement to enjoy the exclusive time and attention of the key-worker without any need for him to demand staff input by resorting to negative behaviour. The adult is seen to be reliable and caring, both in the giving of whole-hearted, one-to-one attention, and in the provision of the pre-planned selection of materials for the session. The use of art or craft materials have a further benefit, as they enable the professional to work at the student's emotional rather than chronological age. Work can be ongoing, and this continuation of shared creativity can form the basis of what Miller (2005) terms 'nourishing communication'.

The first-hand knowledge of the student gained by the key-worker in these hours will inform the planning of the young person's overall support package. Decisions about a 'whole school approach' to the needs of this particular student should be made in consultation with a variety of colleagues from learning support, pastoral care, outside agencies such as CAMHS[2] and the Educational Psychology Service, and, of course, parents, carers and the young person him or herself. This ensures that the scheme will spring from a multidisciplinary stand-point, encouraging a more holistic outcome whilst guarding against the danger of the key-worker becoming over-burdened with an unreasonable level of decision-making and delivery.

The key-worker as provider of time and space

Tony and the castle walls

Tony was a fifteen-year old pupil who was described by his teachers as 'uncommunicative' and 'difficult'. His emotional needs ran deep, and he had also endured bouts of chronic illness since infancy. Over the years since nursery, Tony had been offered various support mechanisms including one-to-one learning interventions and anger-management sessions. Most of these plans ended in frustration and acrimony for both Tony and those of us trying to help him. Markers such as reading-age and basic numeracy levels remained obstinately low in the face of well-meaning schemes of remedial action.

I knew that it was unrealistic for Tony to be expected to negotiate his way around the challenges and vagaries of the school day (see Chapter 2 *for more on transitions). He displayed behaviour which led me to believe that he was an insecurely attached young person, who felt compelled to construct avoidant defence mechanisms within the arena of school. Tony was an only child, and his background contained an emotional tableau of conflict, anxiety and disharmony. His behavioural issues added strain to an already trauma-laden family system. At home, rejection of Tony and his ever-avoidant self was demonstrated by the use of physical punishment and harsh, condemnatory words. As a result, his guesses as to the motives of adults were negative and suspicious.*

I felt that it was no surprise that Tony presented himself in school as a dismissive, defiant and, sometimes, openly aggressive character. His rejection of rules, cultural norms and the needs of those around him began to make sense as I thought about the lonely, misunderstood young person beneath the carapace under which he had been forced to retreat. This young person was in 'full war survival mode' and, as such, he was unable to take advantage of the well-intentioned but non-therapeutic interventions usually offered in school.

As Tony's key worker, I spent time on false trails in my mind, trying to devise schemes of work and learning support structures. It wasn't long before I accepted that this mode of intervention would simply be providing Tony with more of the same sort of attitude and work which had proved fruitless in the past. I decided to run with my intuition and what I knew about attachment patterns and how they presented in the classroom.

Tony's behaviour and non-verbal communication transmitted the message "*do not disturb*". He would turn his back on me and refuse to answer questions or ignore requests for compliance. He had been known to leave classrooms when frustrated or angered, and had gone missing from home on various occasions after enduring bouts of family strife. He would refuse to engage with learning support assistants except on the occasions when he felt able to comply grudgingly with a teacher's request. He would try to use his assistant as a means to placate whichever teacher had demanded the production of a task with a curt "*You do it*", signalling to the adult to pick up the pen and begin work for him.

Tony was immune to blandishments, multi-sensory approaches to learning and computer technology. Confusion and a sense of impotence were left in his wake as he strolled out for break or lunch. I began to see that this legacy was, in fact, a communication about the states and feelings in his inner world. He projected his sense of hopelessness and powerlessness into others.

Personally, I began to experience these feelings as a reproach for not understanding his needs. It was this realisation which allowed me to work with Tony in an entirely different way. *I accepted that if Tony would not or could not learn, I had to assume that I had not yet found the right way to teach him.*

I made a commitment to work with him for two hours each week. This was a fairly heavy level of support which I felt was justified by Tony's level of need. By this time I had decided that I had two key tasks to hold in mind if these hours were to be productive. I had to tolerate and contain my own de-skilling feelings of uncertainty and impotence, and I needed to light upon a suitable assignment to form the safe channel for our teacher-pupil one-to-one engagement. I knew that the task would be all important, both as a way of providing Tony with a vehicle for self-expression, and a means for him to find more adaptive ways of developing a secure internal base.

I was aware that Tony would not work with me until I could communicate with him in a way that he could accept. He was known to reject help from anyone who appeared to take a strong lead with him. Although I felt that he needed a firm, containing adult, I knew that the over-riding approach would need to embody a light touch. His metaphorical *"do not disturb"* sign required me to tread very carefully around his dignity and defences. This young person did not feel safe, and I was determined to do nothing that would exacerbate his anxiety. His need to defend against encroachment seemed paramount, and I reflected upon his experiences of enduring harsh criticism and invasive medical procedures. A subtle yet containing response would be needed to allow Tony to strengthen his boundaries and limits.

Over three-quarters of what is received by each person within an interaction is expressed through body language, gesture and eye-contact. I recognised that as a teacher, I sometimes had the tendency to talk too much, perhaps not always allowing time for pupil reflection. I made a pact with myself to rein in this particular aspect of my personality. A domineering and engulfing teaching style was the last thing that this vulnerable young person needed. I would tread carefully.

I felt strongly that Tony needed time, space and choice. He was not ready to think about feelings and difficulties, which is why all previous attempts at 'anger-management' sessions had failed. I felt that a teacher-directed project, which is often a feature of so-called remedial sessions in literacy, numeracy and social skills, would heighten Tony's anxiety and hinder progress from the start. Our project would need to be more holistic for it to have any chance of success.

I had noticed that Tony often enjoyed art activities as long as they contained a high level of self-direction. I decided that a creative piece could be the means of connection. A discussion with a colleague led the way. Tony's English teacher had told me that she had noticed that he had developed an interest in a particular aspect of her lessons. The group were studying Macbeth, and Tony had shown one specific area of enthusiasm, focusing around the castle at Forres. He drew castles in the back of his exercise book and asked questions about the strength of such fortifications. This was the idea I had been looking for, and I tentatively suggested to Tony the possibility of an extended castle-based activity using art materials. Fortunately, the enterprise was well received and he agreed to plan for a 3-D recreation of a castle if I would help him to collect suitable materials.

This first agreement began our work and a small and comfortable room was set aside for our twice-weekly meetings. I hoped that the arrangement of a room for two hours weekly would demonstrate my commitment to his well-being and importance as a 'client'. I knew that Tony would require my presence but not my instruction, so I planned to work on my own art piece for a Creativity course that I had started at The Institute for Arts in Therapy and Education (London). We would work together, yet separately. I would be there as needed, but not, I hoped, an overbearing presence. The castle would be his creation and his own fortification against adult interference. I collected a little research on eleventh century castles and left it near the art materials but ensured that I didn't insist that these were used. Historical accuracy was not an essential component of the project and I resolved to discard all such notions unless Tony was keen to pursue this angle. I resolved to 'set up base' outside Tony's castle, as I had no intention of laying siege to him or his work.

Over the weeks, Tony would arrive punctually for his appointment and greet me silently with a nod. He would set to work without delay and plan his ideas methodically. He required no prompting from me and seemed comfortable that I had provided a space, the materials and an attentive yet non-invasive style of interaction. Tony's need for self-direction and personal space was great and I believe that he was aware that this was an important part of our unspoken agreement. He incubated ideas by preparing plans and schemes, and I stood back in admiration as he worked.

Tony's communication was mainly mono-syllabic and non-verbal. Eye-contact between us became increasingly important as the weeks went by and I noticed that Tony grew more able to meet my gaze on greeting as the trust between us deepened. I saw this achievement as significant, as previously it was noticeable that he averted his gaze whenever eye-contact was offered. Tony had responded to a gentle and respectful approach and allowed himself to relax and be seen.

Tony's need was for unconditional acceptance as opposed to the sort of approval that is contingent upon performance and attainment. The developmental need was to learn how to be, and he required no targets and unreasonable expectations as to the outcomes of our sessions. Similarly, Tony needed no generalised praise or blanket comments such as "You've done really well", as I believe that he sensed the mis-attunement behind such throwaway remarks. Mis-attunement is the lack of emotional harmony which can result when the needs of the young person are misunderstood or overridden by the adult in a crass or insensitive manner.

I decided to base my comments upon small specific remarks such as "Oh, you've included the stables!" or "Tell me about the draw-bridge". I avoided any overwhelming level of commentary and backed-off immediately if I felt that my words were unwanted or had hit a false note. I avoided interpretation and assumption as well as any indication that I thought that he had missed a detail or failed to complete an aspect of the task well enough. I believe this kind of input would have been received as a rejection and I was keen to avoid any suggestion of disappointment. Tony's need was for a space in which to breathe and create in the sight and presence of a benign adult.

As the sessions continued we were able to chat occasionally about how things were for him both in and out of school. I learned more about the fatigue caused by his difficulties and the consequences that this caused for him as a learner and social being. This knowledge allowed me to pass on ideas to colleagues about how Tony's learning might be differentiated and teaching approaches modified.

I believe that the turning point came in our relationship when on clearing up one day I suggested that for safety, the castle be placed in the cupboard. Tony replied that he felt it would be best in its usual place on top of the cupboard. He went on to explain why this was preferable: "'Cos when I'm passing by, I like to look in and see that my work is there". The poignancy of these words struck me as a sign that Tony had perhaps experienced a sense of fusion with the task and, by implication, with me. I wondered if he had dared to let go and feel the beginning of meaning through self-expression. His admission that he liked to see his work evoked in me a sense that Tony was becoming able to allow himself to be seen whilst remaining safe in the process. The added safety of the study cupboard was not needed as he had developed some inner security. Tony was showing care about something that he had produced. The sight of his model allowed him to keep our work together 'in mind'. I took this to be a good sign of the beginnings of an attachment to the project, and to me.

In our work together, Tony had allowed me to learn more about his emotional and educational needs then any bank of tests could ever have indicated. This knowledge of his preferred creative, practical and kinaesthetic learning style allowed me to work further with colleagues to adapt and differentiate the curriculum in order to reach Tony's 'teachable self'. Reasonable adjustments were made to his overall timetable and support plan. I was able to add some attachment theory into training sessions with Newly Qualified Teachers and Learning Support Assistants and Tony's case provided the ideal focus for such work. The realisation that the residue of past or indeed ongoing trauma is often misconstrued as a deliberate attempt by the young person to bring disruption to those around them, formed the basis of a lot of early discussions. More time was given to one-on-one input in our in-house support project rather than more generalised in-class delivery. Tony's examination loading was reduced to ensure a more realistic set of goals. A referral was made to our in-house CAMHS Clinic, and he received ongoing counselling which was later extended to include his mother.

A link was made with our attached Connexions Personal Advisor[3] which led eventually to a fulfilling vocational course which capitalised upon his interest and practical skills. Initial thoughts regarding the suitability of such a course in view of Tony's medical history were worked through with the help of his college tutor and various adjustments to the content of the course were suggested by the terms of the Disability Discrimination Act.

Tony's need for social connection remained strong: previously, he had been unable to forge lasting friendships. A Sixth Form student who had been trained by CAMHS under our Peer Mentoring Scheme was able to offer time and friendship during break and lunch-times. The safety-net provided by this relationship allowed Tony to become more relaxed and confident within school. I was able to withdraw my presence and intervention level a little as the strength of his connection with this older student grew.

Tony had accepted the castle project as the first rung on the ladder of support. Paradoxically, Macbeth's castle had provided a way out of another kind of fortification. I felt a wonderful sense of optimism that future opportunities would continue to provide Tony with a realistic way to work on the repair of the self. Tony could now reveal aspects of himself without putting up his drawbridge to defend against the unbearable prospect of invasion.

Responding to challenges through developing our support structures

When beginning to work with the vulnerable young person, we need to set time aside to observe and reflect upon the possible meaning behind their behaviour and how they generally present themselves. If a young person is avoidant, withdrawn or appears to display defensive behaviours, it is wise to respect these defences as the student's only form of protection in an insecure and unnerving world. What purpose do these defences hold for the student? They may be a very ingrained mode of relating and, as we have seen with Tony, they are unlikely to be surrendered readily.

Finding a bridge to reach Helen

Helen was a thirteen-year-old girl who had experienced life in the care system, and had joined the school later on in the academic year. She had been described as 'domineering' and 'needy' by care professionals who had sought to engage her in various ways. Helen's presence in a classroom could be exhausting, as she was perceived as being extremely demanding. Peers tended to shy away from her as she would hector, bark instructions and generally irritate them throughout the lesson. Her lack of sensitivity concerning personal space was received as a form of intimidation.

Although her innate emotional needs were understood at some level by her teachers, Helen's negative effect on others clouded the issue as to how she could be helped. It was felt that Helen needed firm boundaries and targets to encourage her to respect the rights of others. Targets were drawn up, carers consulted and teachers informed as to the new rigorous regime. Of course, with the unforgiving clarity of hind-sight, one can see that this blanket response was too clumsy, naïve and over-reaching to ever hope to meet Helen's complex underlying needs.

The scheme spluttered to an ignominious halt as Helen proved utterly impervious to the stringency of the method. An early, much-needed review led us back to the drawing board in order to discuss and devise a far more delicate, responsive and attachment-based plan.

An experienced and emotionally robust learning support assistant was assigned to provide Helen with one-to-one support and mentoring. It was agreed that Helen's tipping point often came when she felt in danger of becoming an unacknowledged and rather rudder-less individual within the hurly-burly of the classroom. Her late-entry into the school meant that many friendship groups had already been formed. We saw Helen as a lonely figure on the outside of already formed peer group clusters. It was thought that part of Helen's over-bearing persona was both a desperate need to be noticed and an expression of her inter-personal anxiety. These insights did not mean that the key-worker would be able to begin work with this student in a seamless way. Helen found it hard to trust, and initially rejected the member of staff with a truculent, *"I don't need it, I ain't thick!"* Eventually, thanks to the key-worker's persistence and non-intrusive support style in the classroom, Helen was convinced to give the relationship a try.

> *The learning support assistant decided to provide proof that Helen was indeed noticed and remembered as a significant individual. Details from the previous session were recalled and discussed, work laminated and displayed and activities designed to suit Helen's interests. When she expressed an enthusiasm for cookery, even though she had never had the chance to try out any recipes at home, the key-worker arranged to use the kitchen facilities in our in-house support project to plan menus and cook a variety of dishes. Ingredients were brought in by both Helen and the key-worker, and this shared enterprise proved to be an ideal way of helping this unattached pupil to feel cared for and held in mind from session to session.*
>
> *The process of cooking together allowed for turn-taking, fun, mutual compromise and appropriate use of space in what is a small galley kitchen. The key-worker would always capitalise upon the chance to greet Helen warmly whenever they met around the school. This courtesy is a small but powerful means of validating both the young person as an individual and the connection between key-worker and student. On occasion, it can be useful to plan to 'bump into' the young person by design, as it is a good way of providing short bursts of sustaining support which help them to absorb the affirmation of the adult. A reciprocal glance or a genuine smile will be enough.*

Helen's intervention was of lengthy duration as it was revealed that her emotional needs ran deep. The ongoing use of the culinary arts was the bridge across which Helen walked to meet and accept the care and kindness of her key-worker. A simple, intuitive approach had succeeded, where an unrealistic, heavy-handed plan had foundered.

Reliability and consistency are vital, as many young people who have endured rejection or criticism fear that you too will drop them into the abyss of invisibility. Similarly, it is important to avoid making premature demands, as these may set the work back by months. It can be disheartening when a young person's progress appears to be slow, but bear in mind that previous experience may have hampered their ability to reflect and move forward. You may need to sit with a certain degree of rejection and frustration, but rest assured that your empathic influence will be helping the student enormously, even if the results do not seem obvious for a while.

Collaborating with colleagues

When faced with the demands of young people who challenge our resources it can be tempting to retreat into righteous indignation. This reaction, though understandable at times, is a professional and personally soul-sapping dead-end. It is preferable to follow Spinoza's advice (1677) and simply try to 'understand', rather than 'wax indignant'. This is best done in collaboration with those colleagues who display an interest in working in an emotionally literate manner. Co-operation as a team, and the opportunity to cascade knowledge as to a young person's relational preferences and learning styles, can create a powerful, mutually supportive forum. The provision of a non-hierarchal teaching and learning group, which meets to facilitate the sharing of strategies as well as occasional heightened anxieties, can be an invaluable way for each colleague to widen their own personal repertoire within an enriching network. The existence of such a group, which meets with the express intention of understanding behaviour and examining ways to communicate more effectively with pupils and students, can bring about important growth in the whole school response towards inclusion.

The use of such a group can be a great help when seeking to work with a student who appears to defy all efforts to teach them. Apart from the strength we can derive from joining forces with colleagues in order to meet the needs of such young people, it is more likely in this setting that a colleague will, often unexpectedly, come up with a tip or pointer to practice which can be shared with others. Often it may be a fairly small observation which leads the way.

Looking at Leon

Leon was dis-engaged from school life and underachieving in most areas. He appeared to harbour bitter resentment towards teachers and other adults who tried to help him. Amid head-scratching and chewed pencils, one teacher came up with an observation: "I've noticed when Leon does or says anything in my class that he surreptitiously glances up to check the look in my eyes and my facial expression. It's like he's checking out the truth of my reaction".

This glimmer of understanding was the starting point of a group discussion which led to a realisation that Leon was acutely aware of the opinion and judgements of his teachers. His sideways glances spoke of a nervousness regarding what might be seen in the adults' eyes. One baseline strategy on which we all agreed was to ensure that we kept a soft and kindly look in our eyes when we appraised Leon in any way. Similarly, we agreed that calm, well-modulated tones would be used when we addressed him, particularly when using his name.

This simple process of sharing a 'thought-shower' between colleagues led to an almost imperceptible change of tack when interacting with this student. Gradually, exchanges became less heated and it was possible to develop a measure of rapport. The sense of hostility decreased, and re-connection, after what became minor disciplinary matters, became easier to negotiate. The confidence which came from knowing that one's colleagues were using the same strategies was a welcome support in building bridges with Leon.

Being kind

Mistakes will form part of the process, and we need to be gentle with ourselves and the student when things don't go to plan. Our ability to tap into our own well-spring of forgiveness and kindness in the face of challenge will strengthen with practice, and is a fine way of modelling compassionate responses to the student. The ability to offer repair after the rupture of relationship will enable the young person to discern that negativity can be withstood and overcome. This will be the beginning of a sense of resilience, which will help the student to develop a belief that they will be able to face subsequent difficulty. To allow oneself to feel and process strong emotion, either alone or in the presence of others, is a strong indicator of the young person's growing capacity for attachment and emotional health.

Sroufe (2005) provides compelling evidence that:

…when children change in positive ways following periods of difficulty, we often find either increased supports or decreased stress, or both.

(p. 227)

I am in no doubt that this advice holds good for teachers, too.

It is this fine balance between challenges faced and support given that must be found. Focusing narrowly upon the details of the young person's presenting problems will only ever provide half a story, unless we also look to find out what is being communicated through their behaviour to those best-placed to understand.

In summary

- Look beyond the worrying and difficult behaviours of the young person towards the underlying reasons that might be driving the behaviour. What 'advantage' might be being gained through these defence mechanisms?

- Provide an appropriate key-worker for the student who will champion his cause and act as an attachment figure within the school. This person will manage the course of the various interventions and intercede as appropriate

- View all the school's resources and those of outside agencies, such as youth work providers and the Educational Psychology Service, as a potential tapestry of support

- Adjustment to the shape of the student's week, by putting in place well-timed therapeutic sessions, study skills lesson, work-experience placement or Connexions appointment, will make all the difference to their perspective of the demands of school-life. Supported 'time-out' will enable the student to engage more positively in a social sense as well

- Look for ways to meet the young person's more practical needs. A comfortable and relaxing working environment, breakfast club, items of spare equipment and the provision of drinking water help to ensure that the individual feels valued and cared for. Advocacy in times of trouble both in and out of school will confirm that you are prepared to stand beside them

(continues ...)

- When working one-to-one, remember that sometimes 'less is more'. It may be that the only way to relate when communication seems blocked is non-verbally. Use art activities and mind-mapping study-skills techniques. Play games which require turn-taking without too much strategy, such as word-games and role-play: watch a film together or use music as stimulus. Your calm and affirming presence may be all that the young person is able to absorb at this time. When the relationship is established, the possibility of supporting the student's personal or curriculum needs will present itself

- Network and share any teaching and learning strategies which prove successful, such as pointers to practice regarding effective communication, preferred modes of support, useful templates for the scaffolding of written pieces and differentiated task sheets

- If necessary, hold a meeting of all who teach and support the student to disseminate ideas and thoughts as to suitable approaches. This will act as a 'collective brain' to think about the young person's needs, and allow colleagues to help each other towards a mindful appraisal of the way forward. This collaborative response will serve to provide a sense of the strength of the support network holding the vulnerable young person (*And see p.53 for more on creating the 'Team Aound the Child'*)

- Be kind and develop a light touch with yourself, colleagues and the young people with whom you work

Bibliography

Batmanghelidjh, C. (2006) *Shattered Lives* London: Jessica Kingsley Publishers
Bowlby, J. (1979) *The Making and Breaking of Affectional Bonds* London: Brunner-Routledge

Gerhardt, S. (2004) *Why Love Matters* East Sussex: Routledge
Guntrip, H. (1971) *Psychoanalytic Theory, Therapy and the Self* London: Basic Books
Geddes, H. (2006) *Attachment in the Classroom: The links between children's early experience, emotional well-being and performance in school* London: Worth Publishing

Hartley-Brewer, E. (2000) *Self-Esteem for Boys* London: Vermillion
Hartley-Brewer, E. (2000) *Self-Esteem for Girls* London: Vermillion
Hughes, D. A. (2006) *Building the Bonds of Attachment* Northvale, New Jersey: Jason Aronson Inc.

Jones, A. (1998) *Activities that Build Self-Esteem* Richland: Rec. Room Publishing

McGrath, M. (1998) *The Art of Teaching Peacefully* London: Fulton
Miller, A. (2005) *The Body Never Lies* New York: WW Norton

Spinoza, B. (1677) *Tractatus Politicus*
Sroufe, L. A. (2005) *The Development of the Person* New York: Guildford
Sunderland, M. (2001, 2003) *Stories for Troubled Children Series (storybooks and guides)* Milton Keynes: Speechmark

NOTES

[1] **SENCO -** Special Educational Needs Co-ordinator
[2] **CAMHS -** Child and Adolescent Mental Health Service
[3] **Connexions Personal Advisor -** support and advice given to vulnerable young people on careers, education and lifestyle

Principles of attachment and intersubjectivity

Still relevant in relating with adolescents

Daniel A Hughes PhD

How do we influence adolescents - we teachers, mentors, therapists, support workers or youth workers - to choose pathways in life that will lead to satisfaction and success, when many of these same adolescents have long since lost trust that adults have either the knowledge or desire to make a positive difference in their lives? So often, adolescents perceive adults - rightly or wrongly - as wanting to control them, wanting to change them, and wanting to exert power over them. So often, adolescents perceive adults as being motivated by getting paid, getting status, or having an easier time if they can make the adolescent 'be good'. Those perceptions cause the adolescent to lack any confidence that this relationship might be different.

Jasmine was 14 and had no use for adults. She had been abused by her biological parents for years and then received various levels of care in a number of foster homes and residential facilities. In response, she demonstrated rage, rather than fear or despair, to her foster carers, residential support workers, teachers and therapists. Her habitual angry and defiant behaviours led to many foster placements and exclusions from school. Adults were now perceiving her as tough and cold, 'difficult' and possibly even 'hopeless'. Her emotional and behavioural 'problems' had begun to define her in the eyes of others.

Of course she would avoid engaging adults who would perceive her in that way. If she could not avoid them, she would verbally attack and defy them. Their perceptions of her only confirmed her own assumptions that she was 'bad', that the abuse that she experienced as a child was most likely deserved.

Sarah was Jasmine's fifth and latest therapist, and Jasmine was only seeing her because she knew that if she refused to see her therapist she would have to move to another foster home. She reluctantly agreed to meet with Sarah but she had no intention of allowing her to get to know her. When Sarah asked to hear her story, Jasmine told her to read "the f***in' file". Sarah said that she wanted to understand Jasmine's experience of her life, not just read the events that happened. Jasmine told her to read an autobiography that her last therapist had 'made' her write. Sarah asked for her to bring it to the next session and Jasmine reluctantly agreed.

Early in the next session, Sarah began to read her autobiography in Jasmine's presence. As the she read page after page of stark horror, Sarah said nothing. Her eyes watered and she periodically looked at Jasmine who was watching her intently. As she approached the end of the story, Sarah began to quietly cry. She again looked at Jasmine, who was also crying. They stared at each other for some moments until Sarah left her chair and sat next to Jasmine. She put her arm around her and Jasmine rested her head on Sarah's shoulder and they cried together.

Sarah was able to have a significant positive impact on Jasmine over the course of the next eighteen months of meeting regularly. She was only able to do so because she first let Jasmine - and her life - have an impact on her. Sarah experienced the vulnerability, betrayal, despair, and pain of Jasmine's life. She experienced - she discovered - the frightened young child who lived within the 'cold and tough' adolescent, and she related to this person with care and compassion while relating to

Jasmine's 'toughness' with understanding and respect. Her tears were not a technique, nor were they part of her 'job'. Her tears showed her willingness to enter into - and experience - Jasmine's life with her, as well as her strength and commitment to do so. What Sarah was able to experience and clearly communicate about her, Jasmine was now able to experience about herself. With Sarah's empathy and strength, Jasmine did not have to hide from her vulnerable parts behind angry and defiant behaviours.

This example may be more dramatic than most, but the basic process of relationship - of an attachment relationship - that made the difference with Jasmine and Sarah is the same process that is crucial in being able to positively influence the adolescents in our care. Attachment relationships are founded upon safety. The attachment figure is perceived as someone to whom one can go when frightened or in trouble. When with one's attachment figure, one is safe. Safety is the foundation of the relationship, but attachment offers more. With safety, the adolescent is now safe-to-explore. The adolescent can explore his life, his past, his present, and his future. He can begin to identify his thoughts, feelings, wishes, and intentions and to make sense of them all. He can discover who he is under his 'problems'. He can discover his strengths that developed along with his 'symptoms', often in response to his trauma. He can discover these within the safety of his relationship with his attachment figure, but also within the perceptions of his attachment figure. He begins to see himself from a new perspective, as he compares his attachment figure's perspective with his own old one and integrates one that is new and more hopeful.

Human beings, from infancy through old age, explore the world in significant ways through their experience of the experience of the significant people in their lives. This is most obvious with children and youth but it exists as well throughout adulthood.

This process is known as 'intersubjectivity', and refers to the impact that a person's subjective experience has on the subjective experience of the other and vice versa. Both individuals have to be impacted by the experience or it is not intersubjective. One can tell if he is having an impact on another person through the nonverbal expressions that are occurring during the interaction. The impact that one is having on another is evident in his facial expressions, eye gaze, voice prosody, gestures, and posture. Those nonverbal expressions occur in synchrony with one's own similar expressions.

However, these do not simply reflect imitations of one another. The physical expressions reflect the experience of the inner life of the person - his thoughts, feelings, and intentions that are active during the experience. During an intersubjective experience the nonverbal expressions are reciprocal and contingent. Those expressed by one are matched with - congruent with - the expressions of the other. With matched emotional states (attunement), focus of attention (joint awareness), and intentions (a co-operative stance of congruent motives), the interaction is intersubjective. In this joint state, individuals can have the greatest influence on one another. In such states, an adolescent is the most receptive to being influenced by his teacher, mentor, guardian, or therapist.

While intersubjectivity is most often used to describe the relationship between an adult and baby, it is just as applicable and highly relevant in describing a relationship between an adult and adolescent. Within the nature of intersubjectivity, the relationship is nourished and enhanced while at the same time, the independence strivings of the adolescent are also perceived and valued. An attitude that facilitates an intersubjective stance - playfulness, acceptance, curiosity, and empathy (PACE) - communicates the value of both relationship and autonomy. The autonomy of the adolescent does not have to be compromised in order to maintain a relationship with the adult. In fact, the adult is conveying through PACE that his intention is to come to deeply know, accept, and value the adolescent, joining with him in areas of his life-story that are stressful, confusing, or full of conflict and shame.

Initiating and maintaining the relationship

The beginning of any relationship will often greatly determine how successfully it will develop. Too often those who hope to influence adolescents do so without regard to the importance and nature of the intersubjective experience. Errors in that initial approach frequently involve some of the following features.

→ Adolescents tend to experience events affectively with a high degree of immediacy and intensity, characterised by strong emotional expressions. When adults respond in a calm, quiet, and rational manner, the adolescent often experiences a lack of understanding as if the adult is speaking another language. He just *"doesn't get it!"*

→ The adolescent's attention is often focused on something different than that which the adult is focused on. The adolescent is likely to want to focus on something practical, of interest, and in the 'here-and-now'. The adult wants to focus on a problem, or a long-term goal. When the focus of attention is different, the adult often tries to resolve the conflict by giving the teenager a lecture regarding the importance of the issues that the adult wants to discuss and the importance of the specific goals. The fact that lectures seldom elicit focused attention tends to be overlooked.

→ Often the adult's intentions for the meeting differ from the intention of the adolescent, so there is a lack of a cooperative stance. The adolescent is often present because he 'has to be' or there will be some less desirable consequence. He often experiences the adult as being motivated to fix him, rescue him, choose goals for him or maintain control over him. He is not likely to have a complementary motive that would elicit cooperation. Even when the adult believes that his intentions are in the adolescent's 'best interests', the adolescent is likely to believe fundamentally that his 'best interests' are to make his own decisions.

These three features represent a failure to attain an intersubjective experience (joint affect, attention, and intentions). Other difficulties also arise to make the relationship even less able to affect the adolescent's thoughts, feelings, or actions. These include:

→   The adult focuses on technique in his interaction and/or believes that his professional stance precludes being affected by the adolescent. The adult strives to remain distant, 'objective', and professional, all of which leads the adolescent toward avoiding the interaction. As the adolescent moves toward adulthood, he is often desperate to experience himself as having an impact on another person. When he is not able to have an impact - for good or bad - he feels like a child, something that he strongly resists. He is very likely to choose having a negative impact on the adult if he is not able to have a positive impact.

→   The adult focuses on the rules and appropriate behaviours without putting effort into discovering who the adolescent is, what he wants, likes, feels, and thinks. Or, while making an effort to get to know the adolescent's inner life, he then proceeds to evaluate what he is told as to its level of maturity and whether it is 'right' or 'wrong'. Quickly the adolescent stops sharing his inner life.

Intersubjective principles facilitate the development of a relationship with an adolescent much more successfully than the approach outlined above. These principles are also central to how adults relate with babies and children as well as to how they relate with their best friends.

✔ MATCHING

If an adult *matches* the adolescent's nonverbal expression of his affective state, the adolescent is likely to experience the adult as truly understanding and responding to his inner life of thoughts, feelings, intentions, perceptions, memories, values, and judgments. The adult does not have to agree with the adolescent's expressions for the adolescent to experience 'he gets it.' The affective expression conveys the intensity, importance, and immediacy of his communication. The verbal content of his expression or the specific emotion that he is experiencing is not what is matched. Rather, the adult matches the rhythm and intensity of the adolescent's expression of his emotion and thoughts. For example, the adolescent raises his voice and speaks rapidly, saying: *"You'll never understand what I want to do with my time!"*

When the adult replies with a similar degree of intensity and rhythm in his voice: *"OK! I get it why you don't want to tell me anything! Then help me to understand!"* The adolescent is likely to continue the conversation and to experience the adult's acceptance about how important it is for the adolescent to be understood and how skeptical the adolescent is that this will happen. If the adult had slowly and calmly replied, *"OK. I get it why you don't want to tell me anything. Then help me to understand"* - the adolescent would not experience him as being genuine but rather interpret his statement as reflecting a technique, to hear what his wishes are so that he might change him.

Matching the affective expressions - and not the specific emotion - is known as 'attunement' and represents a central component of communication that enables a person to feel 'felt', and to experience the other as wanting to get to know him without judgment or trying to change him. Attunement conveys acceptance and interest and it leaves one feeling safe in the relationship without having to defend the 'self' from someone who is dissatisfied with it. The person needs to feel that his self is respected and accepted before he will even consider allowing another to try to influence him to consider changing his behaviour.

In the following example the mentor speaks with a similar degree of intensity and rhythm in her voice to that expressed by the adolescent. This maintains the flow of the dialogue, and enables the adolescent to experience the adult's commitment to her as being genuine and her interest as being similar to her own, regardless of any differences in their perspectives.

Meg (mentor)   So what happened anyway to get you suspended for two days?

Tracy   Old Mrs. Simpson just won't let things go. I wanted to ask Judy what she was planning to wear to the game and you'd think that I was breaking some law

Meg   So you said some things that you shouldn't have?

Tracy   Are you going to the game?

Meg   I was thinking that I might but I have to get some work done first

Tracy   The biggest game of the year! Just ditch the work!

Meg   Nice idea if I can get away with it. Wait! I still want to know what got you the suspension?

Tracy   I don't know! She just found something to give me a hard time over

Meg   You know! What was it?

Tracy   What's the big deal about talking to my friend?

Meg   You weren't suspended for talking to your friend! What was it?

Tracy   It doesn't matter!

Meg   Of courses it matters to you, Tracy! I'm nagging you about it because this is the third time you've been suspended this year! And each time for about the same reason!

Tracy   Nothing will get me to go to the game now! I really wanted to go, maybe I can sneak in the back door!

Meg   I wish you could go! And no, I don't see how you can!

Tracy   Yeah, that old bag!

Meg   Is that what you called her?

Tracy   Yeah, I did, before I called her a bitch. And she acts like it!

Meg   Ah! Now I see why you got suspended!

Tracy   So you're taking her side! I can't even talk to anyone!

Meg   I'm taking the side of a great person who I wish was able to go to the biggest game of the year with her friends!

Tracy   So you'll tell the Head!

Meg   No, Tracy, but I'll try to figure out with you what makes it so hard to manage your anger when someone says or does something that you don't like!

Tracy   Thanks! Wow! I had a right to be angry! I was just talking!

Meg   Maybe to be angry, but not to call her an old bag and a bitch!

Tracy   I wouldn't have if she just let me finish talking with Judy!

Meg   So it's her fault now!

Tracy   She leaves me alone, I leave her alone

Meg   And you're not going to the game! You're hurting yourself! And I'm on your side! Trying to find a way that you stop hurting yourself!

Tracy   I'm not hurt! I don't care if I go or not!

Meg   Of course you care! And I care! And your friends care! And I want you to be able to decide if you want to hurt yourself or not - call someone a bitch or not! Not react every time someone 'makes' you angry. You need to be in charge of your anger and you're not if you hurt yourself when you express it!

Tracy   Maybe I don't want to!

Meg   Then maybe you'll be getting angry at me when I tell you I don't believe you! I think that you want to be more in charge of your life! Being able to live with the rules that you might not like in order to have a life that you do like!

Tracy   And let people boss me around?

Meg   And let people tell you to follow the rules without calling them a bitch!

Tracy   Why should I? She treats me bad, I'll treat her bad

Meg   That's what this is about? She's a bit bossy with you so you hurt yourself!

Tracy   I didn't hurt myself!

Meg   You knew that the 'bitch' word would cause you trouble! So who is
        being hurt now for what happened? You or Mrs. Simpson?

Tracy   Everyone listens to that old bag and not the students

Meg   And I'm listening to you! Are you listening to me?! I don't like you
        hurting yourself! You're worth more than this!

Tracy   Tell that to her!

Meg   I'm telling that to you! I'm not telling you to get a lid on your mouth
        to help Mrs.Simpson! I'm telling you because I want you to make
        it! To be able to do the things that you want! I'm giving your angry
        mouth a hard time for you, not her!

✔ PAYING EVEN ATTENTION TO ALL ASPECTS OF THE ADOLESCENT'S LIFE

When two individuals are truly immersed in a conversation they are focusing their attention on the same theme, event, or object. They are both interested in the same topic for discussion. Then each one's perspective and experience of an event is able to influence and be influenced by the other's perspective and experience of it.

In relating with an adolescent, it is crucial to communicate that the adult is making a genuine effort to fully understand the adolescent's perspective before presenting his own. For the adult to express his perspective without fully listening to the other precludes the experience of reciprocity in the relationship and generates defensiveness and withdrawal in the adolescent. When the adult is spending more time listening and less time talking, the adolescent is likely to spend more time listening to what the adult wants to say.

It is crucial to establish joint attention before making any effort to influence the adolescent. This may be difficult when the adolescent is not interesting in attending to a particular theme or event. This is often the case when the adult wants to attend to a particular problem, goal, or rule-breaking action. As the adolescent resists that discussion and the adult pushes it, sometimes an active defiance or anger emerges, while at other times a passive, minimal focus of attention results. In either case, the adult's ability to influence the inner life of the adolescent is small. He may obtain short term behavioural compliance, but anything more lasting or meaningful is unlikely without reciprocal, joint attention.

When the adolescent resists attending to the adult's focus of attention, it is more effective to follow the adolescent's attention than to try to force him to follow the adult's attentional preference. Once the rhythm of the dialogue is established and the adult is clearly interested in the adolescent's story, then the dialogue itself will present many opportunities to introduce areas of concern that the adult might have about the adolescent's functioning.

However, to focus on the concerns only will most likely break the connection that the dialogue has established. The 'concerns' need to be viewed in the context of the adolescent's entire life. The adult needs to be equally interested in all aspects of his life, not just the 'problems'. With no priority being given to 'problems', the adolescent is more likely to experience that the adult is interested in him, not in fixing him. His interests, successes, worries, strengths, relationships, challenges, history and future are all of equal interest to the adult. Actually, he is truly fascinated by the adolescent's life story, and how all of the elements of it are interwoven. The moment that the adult's only interest is the adolescent's 'problems' is likely to be the moment that the adolescent is no longer interested in the dialogue.

The following example represents how the even attention on all aspects of the adolescent's self will invariably have space to include the adolescent's 'problems'. Still, any 'problem' must not be more important than are all other aspects of the adolescent's story.

Jake (teacher)   Hey, Sam, how did the trip into the city yesterday turn out?

Sam   Great, I picked up some really cool DVDs. We also got to the big arcade at the mall. They've got a new game there with incredible graphics

Jake   Glad to hear that! I knew that you were really looking forward to it!

Sam   There's a cut on one of the DVDs that I think you'd like

Jake   Love to hear it! Do you have it with you?

Sam   No. I'll bring it in tomorrow

Jake   Thanks, Sam. I'd appreciate that. You were going to meet your dad there

Sam   Yeah, we had lunch together

Jake   Glad to hear that. I know that you hadn't seen him in awhile. How's he doing?

Sam   Ok, I guess

Jake   Get much chance to talk?

Sam   Yeah, I got to tell him what I want to do this summer, getting a job down the shore with some of my friends

Jake   Great, make some money, be with your friends and have a good time. What did he think about it?

Sam   He was cool. Probably helps that he won't have to pay for anything

Jake   Glad that he was okay about it. I know you've wondered why he just seemed to drop out of your life after the divorce. Any chance to ask him about that?

Sam   Not this time. That's not something he seems to want to do

Jake   Any guess what that's about?

Sam   Not interested maybe. He probably thinks that's history - nothing to discuss

Jake   Ah. Maybe. I wonder too if he just does not quite know how to go
        about talking about times he might have let you down, not been
        there for you

Sam   Why wouldn't he?

Jake   Maybe no one ever did with him. Maybe he just got into the
        habit of avoiding - not thinking about - stuff that was difficult
        for him

Sam   That's what mum always said about him. He never talked to her
        about anything

Jake   That's too bad for him. Might be lonely. Have a hard time being
        close to anyone

Sam   I don't think he is

Jake   Sorry, Sam. It would add something to your life if your dad
        were able to get closer to you. And it would also add a lot
        to his life

Sam   I guess

Jake   Yeah, I wish he could let you know what's going on inside him
        about you. Sad if he's really proud of you but just can't tell you

Sam   Why would he be?

Jake   Lots of reasons, Sam. I know I am proud of you and I think your
        dad would be if he knew you like I do

Sam   Name one

Jake   How you don't let me get away with anything. How you often face
        things that you are struggling with. How you stand by your friends
        when others drop them when they're not 'cool'. How you know
        music - really know it - more than many adults that I know. How
        are you doing - you want more?

Sam (laughing)   That's enough

HAVING THE INTENTION TO GET TO KNOW AND ENJOY BEING WITH THE ADOLESCENT

With attunement and shared focus of attention occurring, the dialogue begins but it does not continue unless the intentions of the adult and adolescent are congruent. Their intentions in engaging with each other need to be compatible. They need to be engaged in a cooperative stance as they interact. Such cooperation is not likely to occur when the adult's intention is to fix, change, rescue, help, or improve the adolescent. All of these intentions are likely to be experienced as an intrusion into the self - a threat to the adolescent's identity that he is working to establish. His sense of safety in the dialogue will only be maintained if the adult is able to convey the attitude that the self is accepted and will not be judged.

If the adolescent is not likely to join with the adult's intention to 'help' him, what intention is more likely to elicit a cooperative stance? The intentions to simply get to know and enjoy being with the adolescent is much more likely to facilitate establishing an extended, fully engaged, conversation. The opportunity to be accepted, known, and enjoyed is difficult for even the most hardened adolescent to resist. But this process cannot be a one-directional engagement. It must be reciprocal if the adolescent is to remain engaged in the interaction. The adolescent needs to experience himself as also contributing to the dialogue. The adult needs to be perceived as 'getting something' out of the interaction too. Otherwise, the adolescent will experience himself as being important to the adult only in so far as he is a student, client, 'child', or part of his job. Just as the self of the adolescent is not safe when it is being 'fixed', nor is it safe when it is of no interest to the adult other than as the location of the 'problem' that is the primary focus of the adult's attention. He needs to experience himself as being interesting in his own right, as well as being someone whose presence and self has something to offer the adult.

For the relationship to be reciprocal means that both adult and adolescent are willing and able to disclose - to share - aspects of self, to have an impact on each other, and to enjoy their time together. It does not mean that there are no differences in what they share and whose life is the primary focus of attention. The parent-child relationship is necessarily a reciprocal one, even though it is the parent's responsibility to ensure the child's safety, not the reverse. The child still needs to be able to have a positive impact on his parent and to discover aspects of the parent's 'self', if the child is to be able to identify with his parent and develop his sense of agency and worth.

The same is true in any 'helping' or 'therapeutic' relationship between an adult and an adolescent. Unless the adolescent experiences himself as being able to have a positive impact on the adult, he is not likely to be receptive to having the adult have a positive impact on him.

What is meant by 'having a positive impact' on the adult? When the adult is truly 'moved' by the adolescent's integrity, or strength, or courage, or honesty, or compassion, or commitments. If the adult is truly fascinated by the narrative, story, and path that the adolescent is creating. If the adult experiences compassion and empathy for the challenges that the adolescent is facing, and the vulnerability that he is willing to convey. When the adult experiences joy and contentment for the adolescent's successes and satisfactions. Finally, if the adult experiences gratitude and humility as the adolescent risks entering a relationship with him or her after many failures, rejection, or indifference.

In the following sequence the teacher is not matching the adolescent's affective state as in attunement but rather, is leading the adolescent - with affect, not words - into a positive affective experience of self that the teacher is experiencing. The more animated initiatives of the teacher toward the self of the adolescent are often able to evoke a similar positive experience toward the self by the adolescent.

James (teacher) Hey, Sue, I really liked how you stuck with that and didn't give up when you were so far behind! You didn't quit!

Sue No big deal

James It was a big deal to me! And I think to you too!

Sue	I didn't have much choice
James	Sure you did! You could have just not tried anymore! Settled for not getting on the course that you wanted next year!
Sue	That would have been dumb!
James	Sue, many have done that! You didn't! Sometimes I don't think that you give yourself credit for your courage and strength!
Sue	So?
James	So I am impressed with it and want you to know it! Why don't you?
Sue	Why don't I what?
James	Why don't you know how hard you work to have a good life for yourself! To get it right - the way you want your life to be! I know that you've had a really hard life but you haven't given up! You do whatever it takes and I am impressed with that! I am impressed with you!
Sue	I'm not that great
James	Trust me, Sue! I've seen many adolescents over the years - you are that great!
Sue	I'm not perfect
James	Did I say that! Sure you make mistakes, but that don't defeat you! You face up to them and keep going!
Sue	It's not always easy
James (quietly)	I know, Sue… I know… and that's what I admire about you… it's not always easy

Within this context - a reciprocal, intersubjective, context - the adolescent may be willing to join with the adult in a relationship that enables him to have 'a positive impact' on the adolescent as well. Once there is joining, the relationship needs to be established and deepened through a genuine engagement that values and wants to be aware of all aspects of the adolescent. Only then will problems or challenges be something that the adolescent may choose to share, and be receptive to the adult's perspective and ideas. Only then will the adolescent be convinced that the adult truly understands and accepts the adolescent's comprehensive narrative, so that the adult's ideas and suggestions will not jeopardise the adolescent's self, or his hopes and dreams.

At a later point in the dialogue, cognitive-behavioural strategies - if they are still needed - are likely to be quite effective. Beginning with those strategies, however, is likely to only elicit resistance and withdrawal. The adolescent, in fact - in spite of words and behaviours that might be interpreted quite differently - is holding out for a relationship that carries meaning for him, as well as for the adult who wants to enter his life. Such a relationship is our primary gift to him, as well as his to us.

In summary

Through establishing an intersubjective relationship with an adolescent, the young person is likely to be more open to allowing the adult to have an influence on his thoughts, feelings, motives, and behaviours. When the adult tries to change or 'fix' the adolescent, his or her resistance to the adult's influence is often considerable. To facilitate such a relationship, the adult might focus on:

- Matching the adolescent's affective state, rather than his emotions

(continues …)

- Holding his attention through establishing a conversation that resembles the cadence of story-telling, rather than a lecture

- Maintaining the intention of getting to know and enjoy him rather than 'fixing' him, whilst, at the same time, helping him to get to know himself

- Basing your communications on very explicit and clear nonverbal expressions that are congruent with every word that you express

- Discovering the strengths within his inner life and communicating them to him

- Perceiving his vulnerabilities under his problems, and helping him to feel safe enough to identify and express them

- Always perceiving the person under their 'symptoms'

- Being willing to allow the adolescent to have a positive impact on you, and communicating this impact to him so that he can experience it

Chapter 6

Supporting adolescent refugees

Developing a secure base

Sue Amey

"The Taliban burst in. They dragged my father into the yard and shot him. My mother told me to run. When I looked back, she had collapsed and was lying in the doorway."

Article 1 of the 1951 Convention (amended by the 1967 Protocol) provides the definition of a refugee as:

> A person who owing to a well-founded fear of being persecuted for reasons of race, religion, nationality, membership of a particular social group or political opinion, is outside the country of his nationality and is unable or, owing to such fear, is unwilling to avail himself of the protection of that country; or who, not having a nationality and being outside the country of his former habitual residence as a result of such events, is unable or, owing to such fear, is unwilling to return to it.
>
> United Nations High Commission for Refugees

It has saved millions of lives. No country has ever withdrawn from it.

Hamid arrived from Afghanistan a week ago, after a three week journey by lorry. He is sixteen years old, with no family or friends in UK. He appears bewildered and confused. He fled the Taliban after they murdered his father as a reprisal for working as an interpreter for the Americans, and his mother feared they would target Hamid too. Accompanied by his Social Worker and translator, he is waiting for his school admission meeting.

Young refugees challenge us on all levels. We are poignantly aware that many are motherless, fatherless, without extended family and cut off from the cultural routes that would have provided them with structure and security. Behind those teenage eyes are bewildered children. Adolescence is a challenging time for those in a secure family, but these young people are often cast adrift in a lonely and alien environment. Whilst their needs are the same as other children their age, their situation both exemplifies and magnifies the vulnerability of adolescents in general. They evoke strong responses in us, from wanting to give them our spare room, to a desire to pass them on as soon as possible.

This chapter will look at some of the challenges presented by the specific needs of this client group, and how we can work to address some of these needs, as professionals working in and alongside education. This book illustrates how the strength of attachment patterns in infancy determines young people's ability to make relationships, to learn, and to manage stressful situations in later life, particularly when faced with extreme traumatic events. However, I am also interested in how attachment to homeland and culture equips us to cope with life's challenges and tragedies. I believe that the way to empower these young people is to use our knowledge of the devastating impact of attachment losses to help us create the best possible environment for them, one which can support them to re-access their resilience and coping mechanisms.

I will outline some of my work with unaccompanied refugee minors in the form of psychological, social and educational groups using the Arts within a school setting. I will draw on my experience of supporting both groups and individuals to highlight some of the rewarding work that can be achieved with this client group.

The premise for these groups has always been from a psychological perspective: however, the overriding value of the group lies in simple, universal principles that may be replicated by professionals with other areas of expertise. Our experience clearly shows that providing the fundamental conditions of inclusiveness and safety can facilitate psychological healing. Our aim must be to help these young people re-discover a sense of self-belief and hope for their future.

> *Grace is from Africa and has been at school for six months. The teaching staff are very concerned about her. She seems bright, but she also seems distracted and her attendance is poor. She has frequent doctor's appointments. Staff have tried repeatedly to reach out to her. She is fluent in English but reluctant to articulate her concerns. For example, she says that she is frightened in her current accommodation, where it is mixed both in gender and race - she has now moved for the fourth time. Grace often disappears from the school day for no apparent reason. The school know very little of her history.*

My aim is to acquaint colleagues, within education and beyond, with an insight and understanding of the impact of trauma on refugee adolescents, and of the needs of these particular young people. It is also to provide practitioners with practical ideas and tools to assist these students to benefit from education in a new and optimistic environment. Without insight and guidance, it is hard for professionals working in schools to be able to deal with the additional stress that inevitably occurs when dealing with traumatised young people. Often those involved with adolescent asylum seekers incur secondary traumatisation, because they feel powerless to help.

Hamid and Grace are typical of the Asylum Seekers with whom we work. One of the schools I work in admitted around five additional such students each week throughout the school year, although most schools have far fewer unaccompanied minors.

What is an unaccompanied minor?

The Home Office defines an unaccompanied minor as a person who, at the time of making the asylum application, is under eighteen years of age or who, in the absence of documentary evidence, appears to be under that age, and who is applying for asylum in his/her own right and is without adult family member(s) or guardian(s) to turn to in this country.

This definition excludes children who are cared for by a distant relative, or a sibling who is also little over the age of eighteen. Typically it is one of the older boys in a family who is sent to 'safety'. They arrive in the UK, often having endured a long and frightening journey, with little or no English, and are frequently unaware of their destination. Many also come from countries where they have had little or no schooling.

Of the three thousand unaccompanied minors who arrive in the UK each year, only a tiny percentage (in the region of 3%) will be given official status to remain in the UK beyond their eighteenth birthday. Most are left in limbo with no decision made for months, even years, or remain here as 'illegal immigrants', terrified to return to the country they fled from and terrified that one day, immigration police from the country in which they sought refuge will arrive in the early hours of the morning and deport them.

Seeking asylum in the UK   Findings of the Refugee Council:

- The UK is home to less than 3% of the world's refugees – around 290,000 out of 8.4 million worldwide (Source: UNHCR, 2005 *Global Refugee Trends,* 9 June 2006)
- Most asylum seekers are living in poverty and experience poor health and hunger (Source: Refugee Council and Oxfam, *Poverty and Asylum in the UK,* July 2002)
- Around 3,000 separated children arrive in the United Kingdom every year, with the highest numbers coming from Afghanistan, Somalia, Iran, Iraq, and Eritrea (Source: Refugee Council)
- The Home Office detains roughly 2,000 asylum-seeking children with their families each year (Source: Save the Children, *No Place for a Child,* 2005)

Hamid has been given status until he is eighteen, but it is unlikely he will be granted full status after his eighteenth birthday.

Grace is now twenty. Her application to remain in the UK has been refused, despite extensive psychological reports by all the agencies involved in her care. The adjudicator did not believe her story.

What do school staff observe?

A typical presentation of an asylum seeker as reported by school staff includes the following:

Poor attendance	Inability to concentrate
Language difficulty	Apparent reluctance to mix with other young people
Lack of understanding, and consequent disrespect for boundaries and rules regarding dress, punctuality and appropriate behaviour	Due to cultural differences, asylum seekers from some cultures can be very resistant to engaging with staff and students of the opposite sex
Lack of engagement with staff	Frequent reported visits to GPs for stomach aches, headaches, tiredness, listlessness and so on

Supporting integration

In the school environment, young asylum seekers often struggle due to the paucity of their English skills, cultural differences and expectations. Assumptions may be made that they will have enough English both to follow the lessons and to socialise with their peers, but this may not be the case.

Understandably, hard-working staff who are dealing with these young people on a daily basis, and endeavouring to integrate them into their classes, may struggle to make sense of their behaviour. It is especially trying to find that meetings painstakingly organised with other services are not attended. Offers for additional help with work are not taken up and endless requests to arrive at school on time, in appropriate school uniform, are apparently ignored.

To help staff identify students who are struggling, the following checklist is a useful guide:

Changes

Have there been any recent changes in mood or behaviour? If so what? General health/well-being? Is the young person unable to sleep? Is the young person reporting physical illness - headaches and so on? Is the young person reporting a lack of appetite?

Mood

Does the young person seem:
- withdrawn?
- anxious?
- depressed?
- irritable?
- angry (oppositional)?
- hyper-vigilant? (signs of hyper-vigilance might include being very jumpy, reacting/being fearful at any noises, eyes constantly moving from side-to-side)

Behaviours

Do you have concerns as to how the young person is in relation to:
- engagement in learning?
- concentration?
- attendance/timekeeping?
- peer relationships?
- any others concerns with regard to behaviour?
- what behavioural approaches have already been tried in school?
- what has worked?

Incidents

Are there any specific incidents causing concern, that it would be helpful to note?

These pointers will give some indication of how young people are managing on an emotional level.

Psychological explanations

Before exploring a group work approach to supporting adolescent refugees, I believe that a basic understanding of the psychological consequences of trauma on attachment is helpful, set within the context of appreciating the young person's cultural mores.   We will look at Post-Traumatic Stress Disorder (PTSD), grief reactions and attachment issues.

POST-TRAUMATIC STRESS DISORDER

The majority, if not all asylum seekers, have experienced trauma, either through witnessing traumatic events, or by living in the atmosphere of fear that pervades war-torn areas, and therefore may be experiencing PTSD.   A traumatised person is one who has:

> ...experienced, witnessed, or was confronted with an event or events that involved actual threat, threatened death or serious injury, or a *(perceived)* threat to the physical integrity of self or others.   The person's response involved intense fear, helplessness, or horror.   DSM IV 309.8 pp.427-428

The most prevalent symptoms of people suffering from PTSD are: the repeated reliving of memories of the traumatic experience: avoidance of reminders of the trauma: increased arousal, expressed by hyper-vigilance, irritability, memory and concentration problems, sleep disturbances, fatigue and exaggerated startle response: inability to modulate emotions.

If a student is experiencing a high level of the above symptoms, every effort should be made to encourage them to seek psychiatric help.   It is as if the past trauma is ever-present.   Freud (1925/1959) proposed that we 'repeat(s) the repressed material as a contemporary experience', rather than locating it in the past.   The individual's whole being has been shocked by a life-threatening situation in which the normal fight, flight or freeze response to danger has not saved them from the psychological effects. It seems that their entire system is disorientated and fragmented, to such an extent that they can no longer trust their emotional responses.

> ...extreme emotional arousal leads to a failure of the nervous system (CNS) to synthesise the sensations related to the trauma into an integrated whole.
>
> Solomon & Siegel 2003, p.180

In the attempt to block out the horrific sights and sensations they have experienced, young refugees and unaccompanied minors frequently find that their memory becomes fragmented and inaccessible.

> Our memory is our coherence, our reason, our feeling, even our action. Without it we are nothing.
>
> Bunuel 1986, quoted in Kalmanowitz & Lloyd 2005, p.16

Grace

Grace's inability to engage with staff, her frequent need to flee from school, and her visits to her GP for headaches and stomach aches were all mechanisms of someone desperately trying to cope with the terror she was experiencing on a daily basis. Grace was experiencing all the PTSD symptoms listed above, and was suicidal.

After working with Grace (in conjunction with the CAMHS team and her GP) for four years I started to learn about her past. At the age of twelve she, along with six other girls, was abducted by rebels to be a 'bride'. At fourteen, Grace had a baby. She managed to escape with her baby, but her neighbours were fearful that her presence would attract the rebels to the village. However, it wasn't the rebels, but eight government soldiers who arrived in the middle of the night, not to rescue her, but to rape her. She had to leave her baby in Africa.

Many adolescent refugees exhibit traits of PTSD, which they find very frightening, and, once their trust has been gained, they may confess their secret fear that they are 'going mad'. Because of the stigma of psychiatric disorders in many cultures, including our own, these young people guard against revealing their thoughts and fears to anyone, hence the difficulties that professionals experience when trying to encourage them to seek any type of psychological help.

From my experience of working with young asylum seekers what is most tangible is their utter loneliness and isolation. Most are bewildered at finding themselves in an alien system so far from their roots and everything that gave them their sense of identity. Their main symptomatology is not PTSD (any young person exhibiting PTSD symptoms which give cause for concern needs to be referred to psychological services), but an acute homesickness and longing for their loved ones, especially, and in most cases, their mothers (*see below*). The devastating impact of this 'homesickness' and longing for their homes and family cannot be underestimated. We usually find that in addition to the symptoms reported by the school, they experience poor appetite, poor sleep patterns, unwillingness and/or inability to engage in life-enhancing activities, such as sport, peer group activities or academic work. These are symptoms consistent with grief, and preoccupation with 'missing' figures and structures.

GRIEF REACTIONS

In Freud's paper *'Mourning and Melancholia',* he describes melancholia thus:

> In mourning it is the world which has become poor and empty, in melancholia, it is the ego itself . Freud 1917, p.254

Perhaps, as Freud observed, it is more pertinent to acknowledge these young people's 'melancholia' as grief, than to label their responses as symptomatic of PTSD. As with all mourning processes, the young person needs time to experience and work through their grief. Furthermore, their mourning process is complicated by the fact that when they fled, often one or more parents were alive, but with the difficulty in communication they are left not knowing their parents' fate. Some are in contact with their families, but it is distressing, knowing that whilst they are in relative safety, their loved ones continue to be in danger and could be dead or alive.

By providing opportunities to acknowledge and make sense of these emotions in the context of a group of people who share similar experiences, their sense of isolation can be reduced.

Bowlby (1907-1990) outlined four stages of mourning: numbing, yearning and searching, disorganisation and despair, and eventually re-organisation. Many of these adolescents are stuck in the phase of 'yearning and searching', exacerbated by the additional stressors of the asylum process in the UK, where they are only granted temporary status and are continually in a state of uncertainty. They are frequently overcome by a sense of impotence. Step-by-step, we try to help them to 're-organise' some of the elements of their life over which they can have some control.

Paradoxically, young people who are most open about missing their family are often more able to recover, given a supportive environment. The strong attachment bonds which make their pain so palpable also contribute to their resilience.

ATTACHMENT PATTERNS

During the assessment process for the groups I run with colleagues, we try to ascertain the young person's attachment patterns, such as their relationship with their parents and other key figures. Schore (1994) describes the crucial role of the mother-child relationship in both the affective, psychological and physical development of the brain, particularly during the first eighteen months to three years in the child's life. During this time, the neurological pathways are proliferating at an incredible pace, and the future structure of the brain is being established. It appears that a child who has experienced a loving and caring environment in those early years develops the capacity to recover from traumatic experiences. In other words, the recovery of young traumatised asylum seekers is very much influenced by their pre-existing attachment patterns:

> Securely attached people metabolise life stresses well, insecurely attached individuals metabolise them less efficiently.
>
> Solomon & Siegel 2003, p.285

Many of the young people we meet have secure attachment patterns, and benefit from support to help them reconnect with their inbuilt coping mechanisms. We may need to 'hold' the hope and belief in life that they struggle to access, or feel that they have irretrievably lost.

The young people who really struggle, however, who present with severe symptoms, such as suicidal thoughts and an inability to relate or communicate their pain, are frequently the ones who have experienced either broken or very unstable attachment patterns in early life. These young people would probably be unable to participate in a therapeutic group until they have had a chance to access mental health services, either through a referral to their GP, who can in turn refer to CAMHS, or counselling services offered by Refugee Charities. A young person such as Sarah (*see below* p.168), in a state of terror, unable to concentrate, or to relate to others, would find a structured group impossible to manage. Young people like Sarah may be better able to access a group environment later, after a period of counselling and psychotherapy.

So, whether supporting individuals or groups, our primary objective is to create the conditions for a caring and containing 'secure base' or alternative 'home' for these young people. They have had everything that their home represents destroyed, often through the most brutal and unjust means. Once this secure base is established, the content of the work done is dependent on the skills and backgrounds of the professionals involved and the needs of the young people.

Attachment and belonging - what we mean by the 'secure base'

Attachment: *A feeling of affection for a person or an institution*

Home: *'The seat of domestic life' as well as 'the place of one's dwelling or nurturing', with conditions, circumstances, and feelings which naturally and properly attach to it, and are associated with it: A place, region or state to which one properly belongs, in which one's affections centre, or where one finds refuge, rest or satisfaction*

Mother: *Adj: To watch over, nourish, and protect maternally*

(All definitions from the Oxford English Dictionary 2008)

These definitions of 'attachment', 'home' and 'mother' epitomise a sense of 'belonging'. The significance of home encompasses the personal, collective, physical, psychological, cultural, social and familiar. Home is where these young people felt safe. Many have had that sense of security taken from them. Home is the 'place' where people who care for you reside.

Mother love in infancy and childhood is as important for mental health as are vitamins and proteins for physical health.

Bowlby 1953, p.106

For these young people, the lost home and mother can never be replaced. However, if they are provided with a space where they are treated with respect and concern for their well-being, they come to realise, over time, that they are 'held in mind' by both facilitators and other group members. Gradually, this becomes a safe place where they can conceive of the possibility of forming meaningful relationships, even in a world so riven with conflict and injustice. This allows them to begin the long process of reconstructing their lives.

> *My eyes remember*
> *The soft gentle hues*
> *Of my homeland*
> *Dew kissed grasses*
> *Caressing morning skin*
>
> *My heart yearns to return*
> *To the sweet grasses*
> *Of my homeland*
> *But fears the sickly scent of blood*
> *Glinting in sun-drenched dew*

SUPPORTING ADOLESCENT REFUGEES THROUGH GROUP WORK

✔ RE-CREATING THE 'HOME' ENVIRONMENT

Perhaps the most fundamental objective for this client group is to .... recreate the primary conditions of home.

Papadopoulos, 2002, in Kalmanowitz & Lloyd 2005, p.115

In our work with refugees, we seek to establish an environment of nurturing, attunement, safety, and refuge similar to that experienced by the child in a securely attached setting. Children have powerful relational needs: for emotional security, they need to experience: empathic attunement: validation of their subjective experience: containment of feelings, and soothing from the adults involved in their care.

These become internalised during development, and we, as healthy adults, access these same capacities in ourselves in order to self-regulate our emotional states, especially in times of stress. Many young refugees have experienced the above conditions through their childhood, but trauma dys-regulates them, and they loose their ability to self-soothe and manage strong emotions. Re-creating similar conditions enables the young people to begin to re-access their own self-regulating mechanisms. We believe group work offers this opportunity.

What type of groups are useful, and who can facilitate them?

Any professional who is interested in the well-being of refugees, for example teachers, social workers, teaching assistants, SENCO staff, voluntary organisation workers, occupational therapists, therapists and so on, can run a group. The focus of the group can be very practical, for example,

- playing football or any sport
- making art
- video or photographic projects
- cooking
- helping with homework
- gardening

The possibilities are almost limitless. The most crucial elements for a group is a genuine concern for these young people and the setting of clear boundaries so that all members feel contained and respected. Whilst young asylum seekers have specific needs, they are also similar to other young people and any activities which give them a sense of purpose will foster their resilience.

Support groups for asylum seekers can be run by professionals from any number of disciplines, and I hope that the following principles which underly therapy groups, and the safeguards outlined to protect those principles (outlined in the group rules) can help inform many different kinds of group work. I hope people will feel empowered to use their individual skills to engage with young asylum seekers.

✔ SETTING UP A THERAPUTIC GROUP

Whilst many young asylum seekers perceive school as their link to normality, their inability to self-regulate is often challenged further in a busy classroom environment, which they can find overwhelming.   As an Integrative Arts psychotherapist, working within a school-based mental health project for refugees offering individual sessions to unaccompanied Asylum seekers, it became apparent to me that an alternative was needed. Many of these young people found it difficult to engage in individual therapy and were frequently lonely and isolated. Bearing this in mind, we decided to create a group, taking place over the lunchtime. It consisted of unaccompanied minors from Albania and Kosovo between the ages of sixteen to eighteen, as this age range represented the majority. We took a very open-ended approach, facilitating the young people to come together to socialise and talk about common concerns.

Building on the success of the initial group, the second group was formed and extended to include students from other cultures. In the six years it has been running, the group has supported students from Afghanistan, Iraq, Syria, Iran, Algeria, Sudan, Somalia, Chad, Democratic Republic of Congo, Congo, Albania, Kosovo, Macedonia, Kurdistan, Poland, Brazil, Chechnya, and Kashmir. Very occasionally, if appropriate, other immigrants in need of support were also included. Teachers report that the group has given members the confidence to participate more in the classroom, both in their interactions with the staff and with their peers. Two facilitators and interpreters run the groups, and we have all felt encouraged and inspired by the young people's capacity to support each other. Their preference for a group environment, which reflects the atmosphere of 'home', is understandable, given that many young refugees come from cultures which identify themselves by their sense of community.

We are born of relationship, nurtured in relationship, and educated in relationship. We represent every biological and social relationship of our forebears, as we interact and exist in a consensual domain called 'society.'   Cottone, 1988, quoted in Clarkson 1995, p.5

The therapeutic group offers a coherence and stability which is absent from the necessarily shifting class composition experienced in secondary school.

✔   THINKING THROUGH THE AIMS OF THE GROUP

Groups provide an environment in which young people can work on the psychological, educational and social issues with which they are grappling, reducing their isolation and loneliness and making sense of their emotions. We believe that the group provides a unique setting for young refugees many of whom, amidst a plethora of other stressful life circumstances, are trying to manage their past traumas:

Trauma isolates; the group recreates a sense of belonging. Trauma shames and stigmatises; the group bears witness and affirms. Trauma degrades the victim; the group exalts her. Trauma dehumanises the victim; the group restores her humanity.

Herman, 1995 quoted in Kalmanowitz & Lloyd 2005, p.115

EMOTIONAL AIMS

✔	**The small group acts as** - a reconstruction of the family, where group members can feel supported - a safe environment for students to express fears and aspiration - an opportunity to have one's story witnessed - an outlet and container for emotions
✔	Installation of hope
✔	People can learn how they interact with others and have some feedback about this
✔	Instilling a sense of belonging/reducing loneliness
✔	Strengthening inner resources, including managing traumatic symptoms.
✔	Insight, self-awareness, reflection
✔	Confidence building, self-validation
✔	Sharing of problems and experiences
✔	Discovery of universality of experience/uniqueness of individual
✔	Learning to relate to others in the group, understanding the effects of oneself on others
✔	Ordering of experience. By helping students to form a 'coherent narrative' of their life experiences, young people are more able to reconnect to positive aspects of their past and present, and not focus solely on the devastating impact of their losses

SOCIAL AND EDUCATIONAL AIMS

✔	A place to meet with people from one's own and other cultures
✔	To share and explore cultural differences and similarities
✔	Exploration of social and personal identity
✔	Relaxation/recreation
✔	Awareness, recognition and appreciation of others
✔	A forum for discussing issues of concern and insights
✔	Access to pertinent information and education; the students can learn about the cultural expectations of the UK (for example, a solicitor talks to the group about new immigration laws)

✔ CONDUCTING AN INITIAL ASSESSMENT

Assessments are best carried out, with an interpreter if necessary, in an informal room. We seek information regarding; individual characteristics, belief systems, role of the family, social support, post-migration stresses and exposure to traumatic events, in order to learn more about their coping strategies, risk and protective factors. We strive to balance exploring present-day concerns, finding positive aspects of their lives to talk about, with asking about their past.

The therapists endeavour to gain some insight into early attachment patterns. If the young refugees do not want to talk about any of their life experience it is important to make it clear that they do not need to, especially bearing in mind that at this point we are strangers. Many of them have good reason to be suspicious of anyone in authority, and some may have experienced interrogation in their home country. It is vital from the outset to model that we respect their choice over what they are willing to reveal.

During this assessment young refugees often report: somatic complaints such as headaches, sleep problems (sometimes nightmares), social withdrawal, concentration problems, low mood, generalised fear. The assessment process often reveals that whilst the young people often present with some Post-traumatic Stress traits/symptoms, their most common presentations are depression, anxiety and grief (*see above*). Occasionally, after assessment and in consultation with our colleagues, it is decided that individual work would be more appropriate.

✔ DEVELOPING A HOLISTIC APPROACH

The therapists identified the needs of this group as requiring a holistic approach, which encompasses social, educational, therapeutic and developmental issues. The primary developmental needs of adolescents are identified by Erik Erikson (1950) as 'Identity versus Confusion'. As well as exploring issues around identity, which would arise for any adolescent, refugees also need to look at the issue in the context of re-defining themselves in a new culture. Daily anxieties can feel overwhelming to the young people, which may trigger the feelings of helplessness they have already experienced in the traumatic events which led to their flight. The group can help to contain and explore these. We carefully monitor individual as well as group process, and individual sessions are available to group members. Sometimes these are offered if concerns are raised in the group or classroom setting.

The group follows a simple structure and is run over three phases. Over a period of approximately twenty-five weeks during school terms, we run sessions lasting two hours, with a further half an hour for feedback with the interpreters. Both the interpreters and the facilitators participate in every activity, modelling openness and a willingness to share in the process. A typical group session begins with welcoming everyone in their own language, and sharing food and drink. Providing food has become very important as it symbolises 'nurturing', and allows a relaxed time for the group members to socialise in an atmosphere of inclusiveness, friendliness, and concern for those absent. It is a transition time between school and the group.

The time is then generally divided into: warm up exercises related to the themes to be explored, art making and sharing of images, followed by feedback and closure.

PHASE 1 | The primary concern is to provide a symbolic place of safety (a secure base). All group members receive a warm welcome, share food and drink, and participate in enjoyable 'games' or play. Negotiating agreed codes of practice begins this process. We explain the objectives of the group and set clear boundaries together. This joint negotiation allows group members to feel ownership of the process and models respect for their opinions and emotions.

EXAMPLES OF AGREED CODES OF PRACTICE
- What is said in this room is private and confidential (see p.163)
- We can talk about anything - all thoughts and feelings are welcome
- We are friendly and kind to each other
- We arrive on time and let other group members know if we will be away
- We respect each other and we listen to each other's stories.

Reiteration and protection of the above is essential for developing trust and feelings of safety. This initial trust-building stage continues for some time and is crucial before individuals feel able to begin to explore more exposing and painful material.

Various approaches are used according to the capacity of the group. Much of the early work is theme-based, such as a guided exploration of identity, culture and helping students to understand 'emotional intelligence'. Games and exercises are designed to impart a sense of sharing and fun. Feelings are explored through discussion, use of the Arts and play. Techniques to help with self-regulation (see *above*) are investigated and practised. This can help to address some of the physical and psychological symptoms of trauma.

PHASE 2 | As the trust between group members develops, their capacity to recognise and manage emotions as they arise grows. Whilst a structure for the sessions is prepared by the facilitators and appropriate materials provided, they remain open to the needs of the group and aim to work responsively.

PHASE 3 | It is in the latter stages that group members feel sufficiently safe to explore more intimate feelings such as loss, grief, anger and despair at a deeper level. The capacity of these young people to manage loss is inevitably explored as the group draws to an end.

✔ USING THE ARTS

The use of the Arts, for example clay work, painting, music, movement, drama, story telling, mask making, and so on, is very effective with this client group (*see over for examples*). Often the level of spoken English in the group is poor, but most significantly, working with the Arts enables the communication to stay in the metaphor, allowing the young adolescents to explore intimate and painful material without having to detail the events they have witnessed. The full range of their emotional experience can be revealed and contained, including emotions associated with traumatic experiences which may be too painful for the young person to talk about. Containing the image within the metaphor allows the young person's experience to be witnessed and seen without them feeling exposed.

To show oneself through the medium of a book, a picture, a string quartet is to protect oneself, whist at the same time enjoying the gratification of self revelation.
                                                                Storr 1973, p.57

Using the Arts in group work with young refugees

CLAY: (1)

- In a circle - everyone takes a turn in showing a movement which the whole group copies. They then mime a repetitive action which reminds them of their family life back home, for example pounding flour, fishing, cooking.
- Group members are then invited to close their eyes, or look towards the floor (as many dislike closing their eyes) and are guided through their sensations to find a memory of an item, which reminded them of home.
- In silence, they then make their cultural object in clay. Each places their object on a world map, lights a candle, and say what they want to say about their object.
- Others can make a comment if they wish.

CLAY: (2)

- A discussion about positive role models: therapists guide students through all the sensations to remember their positive role model - how they looked, moved, smelt, sounded and so on.
- Group members then model their character in clay. Each person describes their character and why they have chosen them.
- Others can comment if they wish to.

PLAY

- Exploration of feelings through role-play: everyone picks a card out of a hat with an emotion written on it, for example sad, angry, happy, lonely, guilty and so on, and then mimes the emotion for the others to guess.
- Group painting, based on how people feel in the group.
- Feedback on their image and how it had felt to make an image in the group.

DRAWING:

- Discussion about memories. Facilitators talk about how our lives are punctuated with both good and bad memories, which have a strong emotional charge.
- Using pastels or crayons, each student draws a 'Timeline', a visual representation of their important life events.
- There is then time to share whatever members feel they want to talk about with the group.

MUSIC:

- Discussion on important pieces of music in life. All members bring an example of music from home.
- They play it to the group and explain what it evokes and means to them.
- The group gives each other feedback, to include playing and teaching songs.

STORYTELLING

- Students bring a story from their culture.
- The significance of the story is explored through role-play. Members of the group are asked to enact snippets of the story and feedback to the group what it is like being that character. Themes within the story are explored with the whole group, for example, jealousy, revenge, love, good characters, villains.

✔ REFLECTION MATTERS - FEEDBACK AND EVALUATION

Facilitators reflect on and evaluate the group process each week. The observations of the interpreters can be very valuable in highlighting undercurrents that the facilitators may be unaware of. We also meet with the school 'link' person and other people within the young person's 'system'; social workers, solicitors, GPs, CAMHS teams, voluntary organisations, members of their community, mentors and so on to assess how they are managing outside school. No information is passed on to other agencies without the consent of the young people, unless there is a concern about their safety.

There is time for reflection during the group, which, apart from the obvious therapeutic advantages, also allows facilitators to assess the students' progress. With their written permission, confidential notes are kept concerning each individual. This informs the planning for the following week. When the group finishes, each member is given written feedback, an attendance certificate, and photographs of the art work they have produced (having obtained written permission), documenting the art making and socialising during the course of the group.

In the groups we ran, we provided the young people and teaching staff with tailor-made feedback forms and a 'Strengths and Difficulties' questionnaire (these are used in CAMHS teams to assess psychological functioning) before and after treatment. Teachers report a marked improvement in peer relationships, co-operation and thoughtfulness between group members and other students, better attendance, better application to academic work, and fewer individuals 'dropping out' of school.

Henry's journey

Henry is a seventeen year old boy from Democratic Republic of Congo. The school were aware that his mood was often very low, his attendance was poor and he had problems concentrating. An initial assessment revealed that he was suffering a major depressive episode, with suicidal thoughts. He had fled an extremely violent attack on his village and feared that his family were all dead. His journey, by plane, lorry and boat, had taken three weeks and he had been in Oxford for six months. He had been housed with four other students from his country and was happy with his school. In conjunction with the weekly therapy he was receiving with our team at the school, we also referred him and accompanied him to appointments with the CAMHS team, and kept his GP informed. After six months of individual therapy and a re-assessment, we decided that he would benefit from the group, especially as another four boys from the Democratic Republic of Congo were also in the group, and they would have an interpreter. Whilst at times his mood was very low, he mainly 'blossomed' in the group. He loved the painting, and especially the music.

Henry was offered a place in the group the following year. The facilitators noticed the huge difference from year one, when he said very little in the group, to the second year, when he was very keen to share his images and stories, loved playing the drum and beamed when he arrived, usually first, each week.

For me, his beaming smile greeting us early every week, his energetic ssshhhh-shing of other members if anyone was speaking when they shouldn't have been, his enthusiastic talk about what we should do next, and the look of hope for his future has been sufficient confirmation of the benefit the group provides for him.

What is the role of interpreters?

The role of the interpreters is far more complex than simply 'translating' the spoken word of the young people into English. Interpreters always take part in all of the exercises. They provide excellent modelling, both in terms of their honest feedback, and the hope they embody as immigrants who have carved successful careers and family life in the UK. They often symbolise parents, older siblings or elders. They provide a 'cultural bridge' for the young people between their home and adopted culture. The interpreter's weekly feedback is crucial in tracking some of the undercurrents within the group (and asides between students in their own language), and the cultural knowledge they provide. This reflective process is also an essential 'debrief' for the interpreters, who are affected by both the implicit and explicit feelings expressed. When there are several members of the same cultural group, an interpreter prevents 'chatter' amongst them.

What do the professionals working with these young people need?

The feeling of powerlessness and despair that these young asylum seekers experience can be evoked in those supporting them. Professionals also need support, either from their peers or professional supervisors, to help to manage their own feelings, which can seem overwhelming. Bearing witness to the levels of pain experienced by this client group is extremely taxing, and the urge to help is often hard to resist. Individuals in the caring professions are used to being able to affect change. At certain times all we are required to do is to 'bear witness' to the young person's pain. This can challenge our belief in our competence.

Because the needs of unaccompanied refugees are considerable, supporting them is very time consuming. I would encourage professionals to ask their employer for additional time allocation for reflection and supervision, and time to consult and communicate with other agencies where appropriate.

The importance of cultural differences

The expectations of school can seem completely alien to these adolescents - getting to school at certain times, wearing a school uniform. We have found that many of these young people have had very little or no schooling. This is usually because the environment they were living in wasn't safe enough - many report living under virtual house arrest or hiding before escaping. Other reasons for minimal schooling can be poverty, or that in some remote villages, there is no schooling provided. Most unaccompanied Minors have little or no English and with little education the strain of being at school can be considerable. In addition to coping with these issues, many are in mixed housing with no adult supervision (except for visits from a Social Worker or Personal Assistant). They often feel unsafe and confused, and many have problems sleeping. They are often late because they have not slept the night before. Young males from certain cultures find it difficult to respect the authority of women. This has been a recurring problem, especially in school.

If the child is in a family, either their own or with foster carers, we have often found misunderstandings between school and home. By initiating open and respectful discussions with the family some misunderstandings can be clarified in order to effect change in the young people.

Understanding cultural differences - being 'casual' and being 'rude'

A group of twelve boys from Albania were causing considerable concern for the school. Staff reported that their behaviour pushed the boundaries of the school rules on all levels. They were oppositional, would not 'obey' instructions, argued with staff (usually female), wouldn't mix with the other students, and instead relied on other members of the Albanian group to support their behaviour. They had been involved in several fights.

The twelve boys were living with one female and three male foster carers. We met on four occasions with their carers, an interpreter, a male member of our team and myself.

The young people described how different the schooling system was in Albania. Although most had had very little schooling, they were aware that the rules were very clear - if you did anything wrong you were disciplined sternly. Here in the UK, the rules were much more difficult to understand. In their perception the other students were very 'familiar' with teachers. They couldn't tell the difference between being 'casual' and being rude. Whilst the students wouldn't acknowledge any prejudice to female staff, their behaviour towards them improved considerably after the meetings.

In this instance we felt it was important to involve the guardians to both clarify the different cultural expectations, and for them to be able to reinforce the new expectations. The meetings also helped to dispel the feelings of the students and parents that the staff were 'picking on them', with the inherent implication of racism.

Supporting individual refugees

Running a group may not be practical for many people, but the underlying principals supporting group work apply in both individual and small group settings.

If individuals are given the opportunity to express the complexities, pains and contradictions of their experience, their experience may be affirmed and they may feel that others have a deeper understanding of what happened to them. This may support them in making meaning for themselves. In this way they may effect change in their everyday lives.

Papadopoulos 2002, quoted in Kalmanowitz & Lloyd 2005, p.31

If you are willing to:

   ✔   spend time listening to their concerns and fears

   ✔   try to understand what it feels like to be in their shoes.

   ✔   explore other agencies which may be better equipped to deal with their specific needs (solicitors, social workers, mental health professionals, voluntary organisations and so on)

- you will be fulfilling a desperate need in these young people to feel affirmed, understood and less isolated, which will facilitate their healing and growth.

Good practice

Sarah was fourteen years old when she arrived at the school from Somalia. On arrival in the UK she was placed with an English foster family. She had some contact with relations in Britain who were then themselves deported. Sarah suffered from low mood, and was highly anxious.

She was constantly absent from school, and although she repeatedly asked for extra academic work, she failed to complete even the original work. One member of staff was especially concerned about her, and spent many hours on the phone to Social Services, GPs and so on, but Sarah did not turn up to appointments despite texts and encouragement. Four months after her arrival, she learnt that her sister had been murdered in Somalia. It also came to light that Sarah had claimed asylum in Germany en route to the UK, so she was to be deported back to Germany.

Sarah's depression worsened. Her ongoing anxiety that she would be deported was so great that she ran away and was not traced for two weeks, when she was found a hundred miles away. Despite initial

reluctance (she refused appointments for five months), she eventually
agreed to attend individual therapy with a member of our team (she
would not allow us to take her for an assessment with the CAMHS
team).   After six months of individual therapy, Sarah's mood had
improved considerably and she was able to concentrate on her academic
work. When she had still not been deported six months later, the Home
Office had missed the legal time available, so she could remain in UK.

During the assessment for her readiness to join a group (see above),
she reported strong attachment patterns to her parents and family.

The persistence of one member of staff was of significant support to this young
girl. She assisted in securing the right 'systemic' conditions - a stable foster home,
appointments with GP and other appropriate professionals - enabling Sarah to
eventually feel sufficiently secure to accept the help offered. This teacher's patience
and continued advocacy of Sarah's case with other staff members and outside
agencies paid off, despite many failed appointments.

Sarah went on to attend our group for one year. Despite her previous school
history, she was entered into the year above so that she could secure GCSC's in case
she was deported back to Somalia. Sarah achieved spectacular results and is now
studying for her A-levels a year early.

For me, the greatest measure of success of any work with a young refugee would be
for the individual to be able to express a sense of hope for their future. At the start
of a group or a period of individual work, the predominant feelings of these young
people tend to be bewilderment, loneliness, powerlessness and despair. Hope can be
born of developing the opposite - a sense of control, competence and coping, and the
promise that tomorrow can be better.

She listened with an open heart and I felt my own heart opening

as the water lily opens in the sun

I thought my cries were swallowed by the darkness,

but I started to hear faint echoes floating back in the breeze

My hate roared

And devoured me

But when I found

Fury echoed

In his face

Our sorrows

Found solace

My wings,

Twisted & bent

Delicately unfold

Revealing vibrant colours

Preparing for flight

Into the clear blue skies

Of hope

Sue Amey is currently working on a selection of poems and sayings, some of which are included in this chapter.

In summary

In any relationship with adolescent refugees and unaccompanied minors, whether on an individual basis, within the school setting or within family work, the principles to bear in mind are:

- Establishing safety/trust. If the young refugee does not trust the person working with them, no meaningful healing process can take place

- Making space for expressing and sharing feelings. I would like to reiterate that whilst all feelings are welcome, it is important to make clear to the young people that they do not have to divulge their experiences, as this can be construed as potentially re-traumatising.
By the end of a group, we often still know few details about the past of many of the group members

- Helping young people to understand their strong feelings and normalising them - especially in the context of realising others are experiencing similar emotions

- Showing that young people can have mastery of their feelings

- Showing that meaning can be restored through relationship

- Instilling hope and empowerment

(continues ...)

● They also need to be shown that there is still reason to have faith and hope in building new, life-enhancing relationships, giving them back the purpose in living that many feel they have irretrievably lost

Bibliography

American Psychiatric Association (1994) *Diagnostic and Statistical Manual of Mental Disorders: DSM-1 V (4th Edition)* Washington

Bowlby, J. (1980) *Loss, Sadness and Depression, Vol.3, Attachment and Loss* London: Hogarth Press
Bowlby, J. (1951) *Child Care and the Growth of Love* Harmondsworth: Penguin
Bowlby, J. (1959) *Maternal Care and Mental Health* Geneva: WHO; London: HMSO; New York: Columbia University Press
Bowlby, J. (1979) *The Making and Breaking of Affectional Bonds* London: Tavistock
Bowlby, R. (2004) *Fifty Years of Attachment Theory: Recollections of Donald Winnicott and John Bowlby* London: Karnac
Buddha (1973) *Buddah's Teachings* Harmondsworth: Penguin

Carey, I. (Ed.) (2006) *Expressive Arts Methods for Trauma Survivors* London: Jessica Kingsley
Clarkson, P. (1995) *The Therapeutic Relationship* London: Whurr
Clegg, H.G. (1984) *Reparation: Restoring the damged self in child & adult psychotherapy* New Jersey: Aronson

Erikson, E.H. (1950) *Childhood and Society* London: Penguin

Fairbairn, W.R.D. (1952) *Psychoanalytic Studies of the Personality* London: Tavistock Pulications Ltd in collaboration with Routledge & Kegan Paul Ltd
Feltham, C. (Ed.) (1997) *Which Psychotherapy?* London: Sage Publications
Freud, S. (1917) Mourning and Melancholia in: *The Complete Psychological Works of Sigmund Freud*, Vol. 14 pp.237-258 London: Hogarth Press

Gibran, K. (1980) *The Prophet* London: William Heinemann

James, B. (2008) *Handbook for Treatment of Attachment-trauma Problems in Children* New York: Lexington Books

Kalmanowitz, D & Lloyd, B. (Eds.) (2005) *Art Therapy & Political Violence: With art, without illusion* London/New York: Routledge

Klein, M. & Riviere, J. (1937) *Love, Hate and Reparation* London: Hogarth Press.

Kohon, G. (Ed.) (1999) *The Dead Mother* London, USA, Canada: Routledge, in association with the Institute of Psycho-analysis, London

Kohut, H. (1985) *Self Psychology and the Humanities: Reflections on a New Psychoanalytical Approach* New York, London: WW Norton

Kohut, H. (1984) *How Does Analysis Cure?* London/Chicago: University of Chicago

Lapworth, P. Sills, C. Fish, S. (1996) *Transactional Analysis Counselling* London: Speechmark

Mahler, M., Pine, F.& Bergman, A. (1975) *The Psychological Birth of the Human Infant* New York: Basic Books

Papadopoulos, R. (Ed.) (2002) *Therapeutic Care for Refugees: No place like home* London: Karnac

Papadopoulos, Byng-Hall, J. (Eds.) (1997) *Multiple Voices: narrative in systemic family psychotherapy* London: Duckworth

Rutter, M. (1981) *Maternal Deprivation Reassessed* (2nd edition) Harmondsworth: Penguin

Schore, A. (199?) *Affect Regulation and the Origin of the Self* Hove: Lawrence Erlbaum Associates

Siegleman, E. Y. (1999) *Metaphor and Meaning in Psychotherapy* New York: Guildford

Solomon, M.F & Siegel, D.J. (Eds.) (2003) *Healing Trauma: Attachment, mind body, and brain* London, New York: WW Norton

Stern, D. (1985) *The Interpersonal World of the Infant* New York: Basic Books

Storr, A. (1972) *The Dynamics of Creation* Harmondsworth: Penguin

Symington, N. (1986) *The Analytic Experience* London: Free Association Books

Winnicott, D.W. (1960) *The Maturational Processes and the Facilitating Environment* London: Hogarth Press

Yalom, I. D. (1975) *The Theory and Practice of Group Psychotherapy* New York: Basic Books Inc.

Zulueta, F. de (1993) *From Pain to Violence: The Traumatic Roots of Destructiveness* London: Whurr

Chapter 7

Terrorised and terrorising teenagers

The search for attachment and hope

Camila Batmanghelidjh

A new generation of teenagers is being created in our inner-cities and in similarly challenging environments across the world. To the lay-observer, these young people may seem bizarre, appearing to be mindlessly violent, disengaged from civil society and self-centredly driven towards the meeting of personal needs. These needs can seem basic, materialistic and void of spiritual insight. Secretly, behind closed doors, the public and the politicians talk of 'teenage tearaways'or 'feral monsters', and they may be viewed as eroding the social fabric. Clinicians are none too keen on these monstrous potential clients, because such teenagers break the rules of human decency and paralyse the therapeutic moment through their stubborn violence. Everyone is crossing the road to avoid the hoodie generation. Neither Freud nor Jung could have imagined them. And had they done, would they have reconsidered some of their theories?

In this chapter, I would like to explore the psychology of these disturbed youngsters and suggest new therapeutic constructs which may lead to more effective interventions for this group. As clinicians, as professionals working in education and in the social care work force, we need to change our working models so that meaningful care can be provided for very disturbed adolescents. Having described how young people become gang members, I will look at one effective model of intervention, that of Kids' Company based in London. I will conclude by highlighting principles that can be applied in working with these young people in a variety of contexts.

How are violent teenagers created?

Violence is a public health issue. Amongst children, it spreads and behaves like a virus. As we hear of knife crime and killings on the streets, the nation puzzles over the origins and the remedies. The street (any inner-city environment challenged by complex psychosocial issues) provides a complicated system of attachments which function perversely in the absence of appropriate attachments. Children have a need for affiliation.

Healthy infant development programmes the child's brain with the ability to access self-soothing. A child learns how to calm down and regulate their energetic and emotional life because of the love and care received from a maternal source. It could be an aunt, a mother or a father who acts as the primary attachment figure.

Those early loving exchanges between mother and baby programme the neurons in the front part of the brain thought to be predominantly responsible for calming down, empathy, planning, anticipating the consequences of one's actions and imagining oneself in the future. The neo-cortex front part of the brain is situated closest to the skull at the front of the head. The sensitive area in the cortex is the super-orbital, right behind the eyes. Mother and baby look at each other. A 'mindful reverie' develops between them, in which they both feel and experience emotions in an exchange with each other, and in which, as the mother thinks about her baby, the baby slowly learns to think. Research has shown that the response between mother and baby is profoundly rhythmic and synchronised. In this way, the baby feels that is has power to summon up and engage the mother and the mother in return responds sensitively. Provided they are quickly repaired, failures in appropriate and timely response serve to make the baby more resilient, able to fight and be determined, knowing that eventually the maternal figure will return to give care.

For some children, however, this early attachment is catastrophically ruptured. It could be as a result of chronic substance misuse in the carer, maternal mental health issues, such as depression, or the mother's preoccupation with her own survival due to domestic and other violence. When the mother's mind is not carrying her baby thoughtfully, the infant experiences abandonment which in turn creates high levels of anxiety and release of stress chemicals. Poorly attached babies and toddlers, who have had precocious and prolonged separation from their maternal carers, have poor resilience. They despair quickly. Anxiety can make them hyper-agitated. Lack of love can make them feel emotionally abandoned, empty and listless.

Most children from challenging home environments experience a tax on their resilience due to impoverished attachments. But for the child who has to negotiate violence within the family home, the damage becomes more profound. Violent teenagers describe their lives as toddlers in terrifying detail. It is about children who sleep with knives under their pillows because they are afraid of the drug dealers who burst into the house and ask for payments in the form of money or sex. Young children describe their mothers' head being split open as partners deliver blows with broken bottles, machetes, hammers and sticks. More than one young person has recounted how they choked on the barrel of a gun pushed down their throat. As powerless bystanders to these assaults, they feel deeply humiliated and are catastrophically aware of their inability to intervene. They memorise their position as non-aggressors and remember the terror they felt at being paralysed by somebody else's ability to generate horror.

Some of these children go on to be victims. At times they are held against the walls, physically and sexually assaulted, and experience the indignities of being someone else's victim. Their only capacity is to memorise and bank the revenge. Exposed to such relentless horror, the constant release of fright/flight hormones from the adrenal glands on top of the kidneys means these young children become accustomed to living with high levels of adrenaline. They define the world in terms of victim, perpetrator, top dog and underdog. They are relieved and grateful that they survive the assault, but they are furious that they cannot prevent it. They begin to hate eye contact. The human glance has come to mean a precursor to attack. In their book, the child perceives themselves not to have been worthy of being saved. The disrespect they experienced is internalised into self-disgust. They develop the belief that there was nothing worthy of being protected inside them.

Initially, the vulnerable child is a victim. The memories of the abuse are stored deep in the emotional centres of the brain. Memories unaltered by the compassion of a listening carer have the characteristic of being unprocessed. They are stored as if the entire experience can be reactivated to its absolute lethal outcome at any given point. Smells, power discrepancies, intricate details of violations and the feelings that go with them are also stored.

Becoming a perpetrator

The child, in a state of emergency, is constantly trying to negotiate flashback memories, night terrors and a sense of hyper-agitation. Other human beings provoke suspicion and mistrust. Apparently 'good' intentions bear the prospect of abuse and are tainted by the betrayals of the past. The neglected and abused child has an internal challenge which presents itself in dys-regulated energy and emotion. Trigger-ready to explode, these young people are defensive and furious. They are too impatient and suspicious. Years of abuse has made them preoccupied with being powerful. They often seek victims of their own. A compulsion may develop to complete the abuser/abused narrative by shifting positions, becoming the powerful perpetrator, taking revenge by harming others. A peculiar sense of injustice drives them: *"I was harmed so other people should be. I need to know how powerful I am"*.

And when the victim pleads, they are repulsed. In the begging, the young-people-turned-abusers see reflections of themselves as small children, pleading for help and not being saved. The image brings up unbearable feelings for which the source of the reminder is harmed even more. These are the adolescents who kill without remorse, whose sarcasm shocks the victim's relatives and the courts. There is nothing civil society can do to them in punishment which would be worse than what they have already survived. The ultimate threat, which is death, does not frighten them either. Years of abuse has made them exhausted with living, ready to die. Their passive suicidality makes them brave. This perverse courage makes these violently programmed teenagers the initiators of violence at street level. In turn, they force otherwise normal children to become more violent in order to survive the victim/perpetrator game. Children who imitate violence are bullied by the initiators. They watch their peers be humiliated. The aggressive adolescent creates new victims, spreading the violence they have been exposed to in the intimacy of the family home to the street and to other unknown children.

Both sets of children, the initiators and the imitators of violence, seek attachments to defend against the assaults. This can be found in the form of gangs once the children are old enough to participate in street life.

Twin systems of gang life

Affiliations at street level operate along two systems. One is led by the drug economy with the central drug dealer as a 'remote control' business person. He/she recruits the most vulnerable child, usually a loner who does not have a functioning carer in their lives. The drug dealer offers the trapped child a social care solution which is perverse but addresses the child's unmet attachment needs. Through couriering (carrying drugs between dealers), informing or shooting, the child participates in the drug economy apprenticeship. As children behave violently and antisocially, they get rejected from mainstream social structures and they are further pushed into the underbelly of the city. As they commit horrific crimes, harm others and become a witness or participate in sexual assaults and killings, a self-disgust initially develops, followed by a psychopathic immunity to harm, as they no longer care what damage they cause or what damage they are exposed to. They develop evidence for why society rejects them, and agree with society that their identity presents the 'scum of the earth'. A mixture of self-banishment and rejection by others delivers the young person to the attachments of the streets.

The role of violence

These perverse affiliations are not based on sharing thoughts and feelings. They are predominantly about posturing, acquiring a reputation for being able to cause great harm because it keeps you safe. The right clothes, the 'bling', evidence that you carry weapons, all suggest your status as an elevated street criminal and therefore you are 'not to be messed with' or the revenge will be very powerful. As the young people participate in the drug trade, turf wars develop around drug dealing: a code of honour amongst the criminals paralyses the judicial process. The police cannot get the victims or the witnesses to give evidence because their extended families will be at risk. Violence therefore becomes a substitute justice structure. Misdemeanours are appropriately avenged and it continues - revenge after revenge delivers more violence.

The second manifestation of violence is not about policing the drug business but about policing one's safety and the safety of the family. It is therefore important to be seen to be capable of great harm. Some young people tattoo a tear on the side of their face. It is supposed to send out a message: *"I've killed so this is how dangerous I am. Don't do me anything otherwise I'll kill you"*. Those seeking safety from characters more dangerous than themselves will create or join gangs, the idea being that an affiliation or attachment to the gang will keep you safe.

Fundamentally, the need for attachment always begins with the need for survival. The baby, by virtue of being so fragile, is powerless and desperately reliant on the carer. As time goes on and the contributions of the carer are internalised, the attachment is used not simply for survival but also for personal development, love and aspirations. Children who have been traumatised get stuck with attachments that function around survival. The attachment figure does not get internalised but is constantly needed externally to help handle threat. That is why vulnerable children functioning at street level do not use their attachments to each other in an internalised form. Every child mistrusts their peers but is desperately in need of them. Affiliations are sought for safety but not enrichment. There is something compulsive, controlling and lethal about street attachments. Violence, threats and the victim/perpetrator dynamic all keep the child vigilantly focused on the outside world whilst their internal life is depleted and challenged by the nightmares created as a result of the day.

New models of service structure

Historically, therapeutic services have not been able to reach the very disturbed inner-city child effectively. Twenty years ago, some residential programmes managed to remove these young people and do some effective work with them. But those programmes closed down, partly due to challenges posed by the client group and partly due to lack of funding. As I write this chapter, there are no provisions other than inpatient psychiatric units which want this client group, because their behaviour is so disturbed and challenging, and because of the wider risk they pose (for example, other gang members coming with firearms or drugs to the clinic's premises). The client group is thus often excluded from schools, colleges, work placements, GP's, social work and sexual health clinics because of their explosive behaviours. Therapists are often frightened of working with them, as the intimacy of the therapeutic encounter is also potentially a space where the therapist could be put at risk. So how does one work with such complex cases? At Kids' Company, we have learnt from the young people about the best way of intervening in this cycle of violence. The primary task is to work systemically and across the young person's range of needs.

✔ Providing the basics

Firstly, the basic requirements for safety and dignity need to be sustained. This may include finding the young person somewhere to live, providing bed linen, towels, clothes, food and cooking facilities. It is very important to discuss and pay attention to such fundamentals. Often these young people appear to have everything, yet the most basic of necessities are missing. They also need help with the procedures of maintaining a home - TV licence, payment of rent, gas and electricity meters, bank accounts, birth certificates. The basic paperwork of their identity is not held anywhere safe, an apt metaphor for the fundamental lack of security and stability in their lives. They are frightened of forms, often struggling to read and write. They can be terrified of officials and scared of structured business and public spaces. They often experience normal procedural delays as personal insults and can become furious with workers. They often have a complex relationship with food and sleep. Their chaotic and dangerous lives mean they do not follow a rhythm of eating and sleeping. They cannot tell when they are hungry and they go for prolonged periods of time without food or drink. They have erratic sleeping patterns and may be using substances to help them achieve calm and rest. This, in turn, keeps them in touch with the criminal world. They will need help to regulate their eating and sleeping patterns.

✔ Providing a channel for energy

The next phase of the challenge presents itself in their need for risk. Once they have been made safe they are baffled by the calm around them, within which they feel bizarre and misplaced. Their 'addiction' to danger propels them to create and seek risk. Often they have found their soothing through being battered or battering others. It is therefore very important to put in place some high-risk activities which enables them to channel the intensity of their energy.

They require a lot of movement and intensive activity. Initially, however, they do not do well in teams. So sporting activities with an instructor who can provide them with an attachment experience but also give them high-energy activity is a good start. Our gym instructor, who had no therapeutic qualifications but was a black belt martial arts specialist, was engaging the most dangerous young people who would turn up daily for his gym sessions.

✔ A route towards self-regulation

As the need for intensity is appropriately afforded, we next introduce an outlet for the next phase, that of achieving self-regulation of energy and emotion. This is achieved through therapeutic touch. It could be through massage, reflexology, osteopathy and the body therapies (for example reiki). Our experience showed that the young people did not like acupuncture, because of the needles.

As they become more in touch with their bodies, they begin to share concerns about physical and sexual health issues. It is at this point that they willingly attend medical appointments, dentists and opticians to commence the repair work. They also begin to recount some of the physical assaults they have had to deal with. Often during massage, they explain cigarette burns on their skin and bullet and knife marks, as well as injuries caused by belts and whips. It is therefore very important for the body therapists to be supervised psychotherapeutically on a weekly basis as they are the first port of call for peeling away the traumatic memories.

✔ Developing trust through attachment

Once the young person has managed to achieve some self-regulatory control, we begin the psychotherapeutic work. This is done very gently on two levels. The majority of our key workers are psychotherapists. Whilst they help the young people sort their practical lives out, they engage in spontaneous corridor therapy. These are moments where therapeutic insight is exchanged in situ and as appropriate. Such moments may last between five and ten minutes, and could be with different workers at different times. It is a collective therapeutic task, not confined to one therapist. Initially, these young people feel safer with multiple attachment opportunities. The prospect of one intensive attachment can feel too threatening and oppressive. So care through multiple attachments, whereby appropriate interpretations are offered by different team members, works much better for the client. But this approach is more challenging for workers who have to be extremely cohesive in their team work. The benefit of multiple therapeutic attachments is that if the young person feels angry with one worker, the care structure around them does not collapse. Other workers can help the young person make amends when they are ready.

Through the process of corridor therapy, trust is built up. Therapeutic thinking is seen as constructive and helpful without being persecutory or suffocating. As young people develop more tolerance for thinking time and internalising their thought processes, they begin to narrow down their multiple attachment to a few keyworkers and deepen those connections. Gradually, the hardened exterior mellows as more tender feelings and emotions are allowed to flourish. However, this is a great period of fragility. The young people grieve, they despair and can be hugely devastated by any perceived or actual failure in care-giving. Therapeutic keyworkers negotiate this period, striking a balance between the inner world of the young person and their ability to forge connections with the outside world through training and employment. After some three to five years of intensive input at our street level centres, which are open six days a week, the young person often begins to show an interest in one-to-one therapy. At this point they may be ready to engage and sustain a therapeutic relationship, in which they are then keen to explore their childhood and its legacy of challenges.

The challenge facing us all

To deliver a systemic package of care, therapists need to work beyond the confines of the consulting room. Their skills are needed in an adapted form within the communities which these children have to cope with every day. Issues of security need to be embraced alongside therapeutic requirements. Bodyguards with bullet-proof vests, metal detectors and emergency procedures are all needed to keep the therapeutic task safe. The realities of these teenager's lives, the neighbourhoods they come from, the dysfunction of their carers, all mean we need to adapt our interventions appropriately.

Kids' Company was independently evaluated by the University of London (2005-2008). The data outlined on p.186 illustrates the level of need with which the young people presented and the outcomes post a systemic therapeutic intervention. The model works. So what can the educational and therapeutic worlds do to in order to meet the needs of these young people in a relevant way? And what will we need to do in the first instance to build our resilience for this work?

Thinking of the work force

To work effectively with very traumatised young people, the work force needs to be aware of its own counter-transference (a useful term from psychotherapy to describe the mix of feelings experienced by workers when in contact with their clients. Some of these feelings may be straightforward reactions to the young person's story and behaviour; some may be a more complex response provoked by the dynamics between the young person and the worker themselves, coloured by both their histories). Very challenging children can 'make' workers experience catastrophic powerlessness. The child's disturbance persecutes the worker and paralyses their potency. To defend against the humiliation of feeling impotent, workers can shut down their capacity to feel. This serves to protect them against pain but also against the potential humiliation of feeling so useless in the face of such perversely powerful children. But these deeply traumatised young people can only be helped out of their devastation if the worker functions like a compassionate companion. So both the ability to feel and the ability to attach are required of the worker.

To be present and avoid hiding or disguising, the workers need to have visited the depths of their own pain, the dark recesses of their soul so that there is nothing hidden to the self. We have to come to terms with all there is to know about ourselves. In this way, we are able to be in the presence of these young people without fleeing. Remember we only get to hear of the intolerable pain that the adolescent experiences. The young person in front of us lived it and was exposed to it. They survived living

The work of Kids' Company

University of London (2005-2008) research with a sample of 120 children and young people accessing one street level centre shows the nature of the problems faced by the clients:

- 84% had a history of homelessness
- 81% had a history of criminal involvement
- 87% disclosed suffering from emotional difficulties
- 83% had experienced sustained trauma during their childhood
- Many are teenage carers unable to manage (39%)
- Young people described Kids' Company's services as being 97% effective
- 87% have been reintegrated into education or employment
- Of those with a history of criminal involvement, 88% stated that Kids' Company's interventions had reduced their involvement.
- 88% of teachers described Kids' Company provisions within schools as effective.
- 75% of children in Kids' Company's schools stated self-esteem as an outcome of their interventions
- 89% of clients stated they experienced no stigma as a result of using Kids' Company services
- 85% of clients described the staff of Kids' Company as being 'very caring'
- 100% of trainees and volunteers accessing a therapeutic training programme provided by Kids' Company described it as being 'very good' or 'excellent'.
- A 2003 evaluation by Crime Concern on behalf of the Home Office identified an 85% success rate in reintegrating excluded pupils into mainstream, compared to the national average at 34%. "*In an ideal world every neighbourhood should have a Kids' Company*".
- An evaluation by Camelot Foundation Research in 2002 saw a 96% return rate to education and employment for young people who were otherwise disengaged. 92% of this cohort engaged in creative and sporting activities subsequent to Kids' Company interventions.
- In an evaluation by the National Children's Bureau in 2001, service users gave Kids' Company a 100% impact rating; 95% satisfaction rating; 90% of children described the provision as being better than other services.

through it, albeit being damaged by it on the way. You can survive hearing about it, but be mindful of looking after yourself at the same time, because the teenager is reliant on your ability to hope. If you despair, then they cannot have faith in the recovery process.

Practical suggestions

✔ To help the young person towards recovery you need to partner with them and share the intellectual clinical property; that is, empower them with your theory and knowledge so that you develop a 'power with' as opposed to a 'power over' intervention model. This is especially necessary, as severely traumatised young people are disturbed by power discrepancies in relationships

✔ Conceptualise behaviour difficulties in the context of dysregulated energy and emotional management. This means talking not about 'morally flawed behaviours' but about opportunities missed to manage emotions and energy more effectively (*and see above*, pp.130-2)

✔ The primary therapeutic task is to achieve the ability to access emotional and physiological equilibrium, so strategies have to be agreed in advance about how you and the teenager will work together to keep them calm and safe whilst working therapeutically. In this context you could talk about self-management in-between sessions, with the young person accessing people in their external life who could help them anchor when their emotional life feels stormy. Boundaries will need to be agreed, for example, when you will accept a call or how emergencies are going to be dealt with. Young people may benefit from contact in between sessions by simple means such as a text - you are letting them know that you are thinking of them.

✔ The attachment challenges in these disturbed teenagers' lives means they find it very difficult to remember the therapeutic worker as a positive 'object' or even to recollect times of appointments. So fun postcards, emails or texts, illustrating that you're thinking of them or remembering key moments in their lives, for example, a court appointment, will facilitate the teenager's ability to remain connected to the therapeutic experience.

✔ Transitional objects (*see* p.40) in the form of a gift from you that is meaningful or relevant to the young person (for example, a small pillow, a toy, a note), will help the young person be reminded of your care. Do not be over impressed with the therapy world's wish to do everything through thought; some children are too damaged to hold onto thinking. They would benefit more from concrete reminders.

✔ It is important to pay attention to the young person's living conditions if they are in circumstances which are too challenging or unstable. They need to be helped to access appropriate levels of intervention in order to stabilise their practical life, otherwise they will defend against emotionally opening up for fear that they won't be able to cope with realities outside the therapy room.

✔ Work with teenagers is bound to lead to outbursts, ruptures and refusal to attend. Before commencing work, agree a strategy in relation to when the times get bad, for example, *"Shall we agree that I'll give you a cool-off period for one day and then I'll send you a card or I'll call you?"*. Discuss with the client what would be most helpful.

✔ Finally, be creative, be flexible whilst boundaried. Expect it to be tough so that you're not disappointed when the going gets rough. And, finally, be brave. Risk is a core aspect of adolescence and you have to learn to work with it. Be emotionally honest without being hurtful; for example, tell them when you're finding it difficult to like their behaviour but remind them that you like them.

Isabella's journey

Isabella's mother was living in a squat. She suffered from multiple addictions which generated a chaotic lifestyle. Often, drug dealers would burst in and assault her for not having paid a debt. Isabella remembers these attacks as well as hiding behind the cigarette-burnt sofa to avoid the bailiffs. There was always a shortage of food. Isabella was often terrified of her mother as she could not predict her mood swings which could lead her to shaking Isabella ferociously or boxing her. A rapidly evolving collection of men used to make Isabella call them dad. Sometimes amidst the craziness Isabella had fun, but most of the time she felt terrified. The history of this terror has left a legacy - dark circles under translucently blue eyes and a skin bleakly shaded with terror.

Isabella describes herself as a child, frightened of adults, unable to sleep, still wetting the bed and seeking comfort by causing lacerations on her arm. When the blood flows from the self-harm she feels soothed, as if violence to herself is her way of comforting herself in the absence of a robust carer.

Isabella is reluctant to admit to these challenges. She reveals her tattoo, telling the world to f*** off. She avoids eye contact if it's coming from others but delivers a lethal gaze, reminding potential adversaries of her capacity to attack. She's broken a few bottles over people's heads. She can feel neither joy nor appetite. She feels flat, passively suicidal, and dices with death every day by taking risks.

For the drug dealer she carries crack cocaine wrapped in cling film in her mouth or vagina. Even though she does sex for money, she's obsessionally preoccupied with manicuring her nails, proud that she's stopped biting them now.

Isabella's biggest problem is that she can't find a reason to live because *she believes if she died no-one would miss her and no-one would care. It's the meaninglessness that's killing her more than the violence. The therapist working with her is going to have to love her so much as to be able to rekindle her desire to preserve her own life, and in the process learn to respect the lives of others.*

Isabella was lucky. Through sandplay her therapeutic worker allowed her to externalise her inner landscapes and by being a compassionate presence, the therapist managed to demonstrate the benefit of companionship to Isabella who had survived through ferocious loneliness.

By keeping in touch with Isabella in between sessions, through text messages, the therapist demonstrated to Isabella how the mind of one could carry the other even if physical absence separated both. Isabella began to risk believing that being thought about by another human being didn't have to lead to being attacked. That being in another's mind could be a good experience, minimising isolation and reducing the devastation of being alone.

When the therapist cared enough to hold Isabella in mind even beyond the sessions then Isabella knew she had been 'chosen'. The fact that the therapist had chosen her to be remembered meant Isabella was not toxic or intrinsically flawed. The first steps towards gaining self-esteem commenced.

But as Isabella became more attached to the therapist she panicked; afraid that the good feelings would be taken away from her and the loss would result in a devastating fall back to her childhood desolation. Isabella hated being at the mercy of someone else's gift because the abandonment could have been catastrophic. So to take charge of the situation, be in control, she decided to engineer the therapist's rejection of her. She walked into the session with a container full of her own urine and tipped it over the therapist's head and then set about squirting the bottles of paint all over the room. The therapist, stunned, lost control and asked her to leave. This was the beginning of many attempts to rupture the therapeutic alliance. It's not that they won't happen, but the reparation of these moments is what strengthens the therapeutic alliance and ultimately leads to recovery.

Many subsequent sessions were spent working through this incident and gaining insight from it. Isabella was helped to access remorse to recognise why she acted out with the urine-throwing incident and, through the repair, deepened the therapeutic relationship between the therapist and herself. It's never easy, but every moment of therapeutic work with an adolescent bears a 'gift'. Isabella has still challenges ahead of her, but at least she has a desire to overcome them, and live.

It is a privilege to work with traumatised teenagers. They have visited spaces of the soul which affords them extraordinary insight. Their courage and dignity is always deeply inspiring. Their honesty creates so much wonderful energy and they will keep you young!

In summary

- Young children who have witnessed or experienced violence may go on to become victims or perpetrators of further violence

- Both the initiators and the imitators of violence seek attachments to defend against the assaults

- Children who have been traumatised get stuck with attachments that function around survival. A mixture of self-banishment and rejection by others pushes the young person towards joining street gangs

- In order to reach and work effectively with these adolescents, the primary task is to work systemically and across their range of needs:
  - basic physical and practical matters - finding and maintaining a home, regulating food and sleep, locating essential paperwork, keeping appointments
  - an intensity of high-energy activity, designed to enable them to channel their energies effectively
  - gentle therapeutic touch, medical and dental input
  - therapeutic support, initially via a team and gradually via an individual therapist when the young person is ready
  - small, tangible tokens of attachment, rather than a reliance on thought
  - a 'power with' rather than a 'power over' model of intervention
  - agreed strategies for self-management and returning to a calm state with support
  - boundaries which are firm as well as flexible

● The workforce needs support to work with highly traumatised adolescents, to contain the strong feelings aroused and to be able to remain present in relationship with the young person

References

Dr. Carolyn Gaskell, Queen Mary, University of London, (2005-2008)
Camelot Foundation Research, 2002
National Children's Bureau, 2001
Crime Concern on behalf of the Home Office, 2003

Chapter 8

Making the transition from school

Attachment issues for adolescents going to university

Ann Heyno

"When I first came to university, I was terrified. I didn't leave the campus for nearly five weeks. I come from a small village, where everyone knows everyone else and the only thing you have to worry about is the wild animals roaming around at night. In London there were people everywhere. Everything seemed so fast and everyone, even the students, looked so angry and unfriendly. After a week, I wrote home saying I was leaving university at Christmas. I didn't imagine I would make it this far. Now I am worried what will happen when I leave."

Joseph, Final year Accounting, international student

Going to university is potentially one of the most exciting times in a young person's life. It can provide them with an opportunity to experiment with being 'grown up' in a relatively safe environment. For many students, university involves leaving home for the first time and learning to look after themselves.

Winnicott (1964) said of nursery school, that it has

…obvious important functions. One such is the provision of a few hours a day of an emotional atmosphere that is not the highly-charged one of the home. This gives the child breathing space for personal development.

p.191

This opportunity of escaping the 'charged atmosphere of family life' can be applied to university. Being at university gives adolescents a taste of freedom from the strictures of home, while at the same time allowing them to go back during the holidays. It gives them a chance to establish friendships and try out new relationships, without being 'watched' by their families, and it allows them the time to discover their own identity and decide how they want to spend the rest of their lives, all central issues to the adolescent 'tasks' of separating and learning about independence.

Academically, it can bring young people exciting new challenges as well as the opportunity to concentrate on the subjects that really interest them. If they enjoy extra curriculum activities, such as music, writing, politics, sport or acting, there are plenty of opportunities to try these out. Socially, it is one of the best places for young people to make new friends and to have fun. Sexually, it gives them the privacy to try things out and make mistakes without their parents looking on or disapproving.

For most young people, university provides what psychoanalyst Donald Winnicott (1971) described as a 'transitional space', and what Abram (1996) calls 'an intermediate zone' (p.322). At best, this intermediate zone gives young people a place between home and the real world:

> In many ways, the higher education system affords the young adult an extended period during which to continue the process of separating and becoming independent. University offers a half-way house between the paternalistic protection and control of school and personal liability of the workplace. There is considerably less structure than at school; work and attendance are monitored less closely, and the emphasis is shifted towards self-regulation and self assessment.   Rana 2000, p.57

As well as being a potentially exciting time for adolescents, the transitional space that university provides also arouses fears and anxieties. Even the most confident of young people worry about whether they will be able to survive at university. They worry about whether they will be able to manage without their parents' or family's support on a day-to-day basis, whether they will be able to look after themselves, or manage financially. They worry about whether they will make friends, whether they will be able to do the work and if they are away from home for the first time, whether they will be too homesick to make the most of the experience. In other words, they worry about whether they will be able to cope as adults in their own right.

Additionally, for most eighteen years olds, leaving school is a time when they are struggling to understand what it means to be independent and autonomous, and as they do so, they may fluctuate quite rapidly, between wanting to be totally independent and suddenly appearing very needy and dependent. These sorts of mood swings, in which parents and teachers can be hated and rejected one moment and loved and needed the next, can be very confusing for everyone, not least the adolescent, who is trying to break or change ties with old attachments in order to make new ones.

Because young people coming up to university are still engaged in this struggle between wanting to separate and wanting to remain dependent, they very much need adults to tactfully guide and support them through the highly charged transition from school to university, to a life of mature independence and inter-dependence.
Beyond all this, the double challenge of -

  • attempting to make the transition from the familiar environment
   of school to the unfamiliar one of university,

whilst at the same time,

  • facing up to the developmental tasks relevant to this stage of
   adolescence (separating and becoming independent)

can create even bigger problems for those young people who are already struggling with attachment difficulties. This group of young people will have experienced the usual moves from home to primary school, from primary to secondary school.

But they may have also experienced sudden upheaval, loss, trauma, neglect and bereavement: moves to and from foster care, or to adoptive parents: several changes of school: even exclusion. Their capacity to form constructive attachments may still be limited, and this vulnerability will seriously affect their ability to make the transition to university successfully, or to engage with all that their time at university has to offer. How they feel and what they think about going to university will be hugely affected by their experience of earlier transitions, and whether they received support from home or from school in making them. These students in particular will need adults around them who understand what they are going through and are able to help.

In this chapter, I will outline the usual hopes and fears that adolescents have to struggle with as they make the transition from school to university. Against this backdrop, I will consider the relevant challenges for students with attachment difficulties. I will then discuss what schools can do to help young people prepare for university, and how universities can work to create a 'secure base' to support young people with attachment difficulties as they struggle to engage.

I shall be looking at these issues in the light of the changing nature of the student population in the early 21st century. In recent years, more young people in the UK have been encouraged to enter Higher Education than every before. This policy, of Widening Participation, (Department of Education and Skills, 2003) has meant that many adolescents are coming to university who are the first in their family to study at this level. Previously disadvantaged young people, such as those with mental health problems, those who have struggled with the difficulties described above, those with dyslexia and other disabilities are now being given the opportunity to study. Others may be refugee or immigrant students, who may have already felt isolated and alienated before they come to university. International students, whose families or communities have put their life savings into the young person's education, may have to struggle with different learning styles, language, and a system of education that seems to them remote and quite possibly uncontaining.

For all these students, the relative freedom of university life may exacerbate existing issues around attachment and belonging, and this in turn may affect their capacity to attach to university life, and to learn. Geddes' concept of the Learning Triangle (2006) between the pupil's relationship to teacher and task is of relevance at this stage in education. Transposed to the university setting, we can see how the student's attachment difficulties can affect their ability to engage both with people at university (tutors, administrators, friends) and the academic or social task (independent study, independent living).

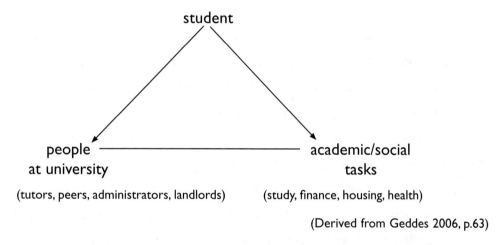

(Derived from Geddes 2006, p.63)

It is unlikely that these students will describe their difficulties in terms of not 'attaching' to the university. They are much more likely to act out their problems through underperforming, poor attendance, social isolation, dropping out or self-medicating with drugs and alcohol. Those students who do come for help may appear to tutors and counsellors to be over-anxious or over-dependent; they may present with physical symptoms, depression, panic attacks or difficult relationships with staff and other students. They may cause universities concern if they are acting out their difficulties. Alternatively, the student may quietly disappear if their problems in relation to attachment are not recognised.

Nineteen-year-old Carl was one such student. When he came to university, he felt isolated and depressed. He came from a very troubled home, in which his father was violent and abusive towards the family and his mother suffered from mental health problems. His two younger brothers were school refusers, but Carl was determined to get a degree and make a success of his life.

Carl came from a city in the North of England and didn't expect to find life in London a problem. However, in his room in halls, he felt so lonely that he couldn't sleep. He was terrified of being thrown out of university but couldn't bring himself to go for help. Instead, he sat in his room at night, taking drugs as a way of self-medicating and trying to ward off the depression. Because he couldn't sleep, he was too tired to attend lectures and when he did appear in class, he was aggressive and uncooperative with staff and other students. When he was eventually persuaded to go for help, he confessed to feeling seriously suicidal. His insecure attachment pattern and his very difficult home circumstances meant that the relatively uncontained environment of university was too much for him. Until he was plugged into the local community mental health team, the university health service and the university counselling service, he was unable to function as a student and even then his career at university was quite precarious.

Young people such as Carl will need specialist input from educational psychologists, student counsellors and possibly psychiatrists if they are to go on to fulfil their potential and develop emotionally. These students are the exception, but they do highlight how crucial the transition to university is in terms of tipping the balance between moving forward developmentally, or standing still.

As educational staff in schools preparing young people for university: as tutors and university counsellors; and as allied staff involved in student welfare, it is important that we all understand what may be going on for these students, and that we find ways of helping them or refer them on to appropriate assistance.

Setting the scene: the effect of past transitions

Like all transitions, the experience of going to university will stir up memories of earlier transitions such as starting at nursery, primary or secondary school. If parents and carers were sensitive to and aware of the mixed emotions their child was likely to experience when they started nursery or went to a child minder, for example (a mixture of apprehension and excitement), and if they prepared their child for the new experience and talked about what was likely to happen, things should have run relatively smoothly. Nursery and primary school teachers' sensitivity to the child's conflicting feelings will have complemented parents' input. Between them, the adults will have enabled the child to feel safe and contained enough to enjoy the new experience and to have benefited from the excitement and stimulation she found in her new world. Such experience will form a positive template for the child's image of what future transitions may be like (including a later move to university).

However, if the child was too distressed by early separation, and her emotions were ignored or dismissed by the adults around her, there are likely to have been problems in the engagement with school. If there were major losses, trauma or violence in the family, redundancy, conflict, mental health problems or addiction, or if the parents were too pre-occupied with their own difficulties to focus on the child, then she may already have been struggling with attachment difficulties. If teachers, carers and parents did not work together to attune to the child's struggle to engage with teachers or with tasks, it is unlikely that she would have been able to settle to learn or develop intellectually or socially. Her view of future transition to new learning environments is likely to be coloured by these painful experiences.

Student counsellors in universities are familiar with the young person who dates her emotional difficulties back to the age of eleven, when she first went to secondary school.

Tina's fear of separating

Eleven year old Tina could not make a satisfactory transition from primary school, even though she was academically able. She had a severely disabled younger brother and a mother who expected Tina to be 'a big girl' and mostly cope alone. Tina was so frightened that her brother would die while she was at school that she refused to go. Somehow at primary school she had felt safe, but in the larger environment of secondary school she felt overwhelmed and frightened, putting her anxieties onto the fragility of her brother. She then became paralysed in her development, and eventually fell so far behind that her chances of making academic progress became restricted. Her anxiety left her unable to separate sufficiently from her family to make the necessary attachment needed to succeed at secondary school.

The move from primary to secondary can reactivate the early anxieties about falling apart and not being able to cope. The new environment may be experienced as strange and upsetting; at secondary school, children are no longer in one room, all day, with one teacher, but have to move between rooms and teachers, amongst many more fellow pupils. After the relative protection of primary school, moving to the larger educational setting of secondary school can feel like changing from being a big fish in a small contained pond, to being a tiny and possibly vulnerable fish in a bigger and more uncontained one. This will be especially true for children with attachment difficulties. The transition from primary to secondary needs to be managed collaboratively by parents, carers and teachers to give the child the best chance of success (*see* Chapter 2) and a healthy template for future transitions.

Looking towards the even bigger 'pond' of university

By the time adolescents have reached year twelve and thirteen at school, most of them will feel themselves to be quite important members of their community. Some of them will be prefects, and most of them will be in a position in which they are looked up to and respected by younger pupils. After more than seven years in the same environment, with some of the same teachers, most of them will have become institutionalised. Whatever they feel about it, and however much they say they want to leave, school will have become the centre of their world outside the home. Their friends are there. They know what the routine is, they know what the rules are and what to expect. If they are doing 'A' levels, most of them probably have a very good relationship with their teachers, who know them well and understand their difficulties, their strengths and their weaknesses. However much they might say they are longing to leave school and home, the wish to stay where they are, with the familiar, will be great. As with the earlier educational transitions, they will be pulled in many directions at the same time. Inevitably, the desire to move on, with all the hopes, expectations and excitements that the next stage brings, will be tinged with the fear of stepping into a far wider outside world that is largely unknown to them.

Schools need to set aside time for young people to discuss their hopes and fears about university. They need to encourage pupils to ask for help when they need it, normalising the need to be pro-active in seeking support once they get to college.

Twenty-one year-old Samantha spent the first years of her life in Africa, living with her aunt. When she was eight, her mother sent for her and she lived with her for several years in the UK until, tragically, her mother died in a road accident. Samantha then went to live with her father at the age of sixteen. When she was seventeen, she became pregnant. Her father made her have an abortion and threw her out of the house. Fortunately, the school was very supportive, and she managed to find another aunt to live with while she completed her 'A' levels.

Samantha did well in her first year at university, but, in her second year, she started having panic attacks when she heard the aunt, who raised her in Africa, was suffering from a serious illness. Samantha was resourceful, and managed to elicit help from her tutor. The tutor referred Samantha to the counselling service where she was supported until she graduated. Despite her panic attacks and occasional suicidal thoughts, she was able to make good use of psychiatric and counselling support and successfully completed her degree.

This student had sufficiently good experiences at school and university to carry her through. She also had the internal resources and some good early attachment experiences to sustain her. Her story demonstrates how important it is for schools and universities to support students who may be struggling. Preparation for university life will be particularly important for young people with attachment difficulties.

Looking forward with a mixture of hopes and worry

At an Academy College in South East London, the school counsellor sets aside an afternoon to help a group of year twelve students to discuss their thoughts and anticipate what university will be like. She invites two student counsellors from a London university to manage and facilitate the session. After some input from the counsellors about the challenges and opportunities of under-graduate life, the students are asked to say what they are looking forward to and what they are worried about in terms of the next stage in their lives.

At one of these sessions, the students said that the things they were looking forward to included: 'Parties and social life: meeting new people: a new environment: living on your own away from the family, and intellectual conversation.' The things they were worried about included 'Cooking: meeting new people: being taught very differently and having to create a different relationship with teachers.' They also expressed worries about how they would handle their money and manage their independence.

MIXED FEELINGS I   CAN I MOVE AWAY AND STILL BE LOVED?

The responses of these young people are fairly typical. Going to university was about to open up a whole set of new possibilities for them, particularly socially, and their responses illustrate their mixed feelings and ambivalence about this. Most students in the group were the first in their family to go to university, so there was no tradition of knowing what it would be like. A few spoke of their anxiety that going to university might affect their relationship with family and friends. They were concerned that entering this new world might make their siblings and parents feel left behind. They wondered if they would still fit in when they came home in the holidays or whether their friends, who weren't going to university, would see them as *'stuck up'* and exclude or reject them because of this.

One Asian student said her family didn't want her to go to university because they were worried that it would *'corrupt her'*. She said her parents eventually said she could go but only if she agreed to an arranged marriage, at the end of her course, and lived at home. What she was saying is fairly typical of a group of students for whom going to university can leave them feeling torn between the two cultures of home and university. Some of their families do not recognise the concept of separation, and see their children's attachment to a new and possibly alien culture as threatening. It is important that teachers and university staff are aware of this pressure on some of their students and help them to discuss it openly, without taking sides or criticising the parents for their cultural differences.

These young people's comments reflect the real pull between the desire to be free and independent and the anxiety that they might not succeed in doing this. The anxieties of young people with previous early experiences of loss and trauma will overlay this tension.

MIXED FEELINGS 2   WHAT ABOUT MY MATES?

This stage in an adolescent's life is also one in which attachment to the peer group and approval from them can take precedence over parental and family approval: sometimes this interferes with a young person's attempt to go to university.

> *Twenty-seven year-old Rick came to university as a mature student after leaving school at sixteen. Until 'A' level, he was doing very well at school. He had nine GCSE's, all with good grades: then he suddenly stopped trying and left school without his 'A' levels. He had a series of low-level jobs in which he always perceived his managers to be less able than himself: this was very frustrating for him.*
>
> *It was only when he came to university and saw a counsellor that Rick began to understand that he had underachieved at school as a way of remaining within his peer group. He came from a working class background, in London, in which few of his peers achieved academically: doing well at school set him apart from them. Without realising it, he had 'chosen' to underachieve as a way of not being excluded from his peer group. For Rick, the price of making the transition from school to university was too high at that point in his life, in terms of his significant attachment. He had to wait until he was in his late twenties to fulfil his potential.*

MIXED FEELINGS 3   WILL I BE GOOD ENOUGH?
WHO AM I WORKING FOR?

As well as having to struggle with these developmental conflicts, there are other more concrete uncertainties that students have to deal with in the period leading up to university. Most year twelve students are offered conditional places at university, based on the grades their teachers predict for them. This puts them under considerable pressure to do as well or better than predicted. They have to work very hard academically, while at the same time, considering what they will do if they don't get into the university of their choice, or if they fail their exams. Some of them may have parents who have put pressure on them to study subjects they are not really interested in, because these subjects are perceived to have better vocational opportunities attached to them. Lack of interest in the subject, combined with anger with their parents, may lead some students to underachieve academically.

These additional and very real pressures make the task of separating from parents and school and emotionally attaching to the next stage, a precarious one. It may push some young people into a position where they cling to the familiar as a way of protecting themselves from possible rejection if they fail their exams, or against the pain of separation. Some adolescents spend hours watching television or playing video games instead of working, as a way of defending themselves against this fear of failure. They may think that if they don't try, they won't really be failing. They can falsely reassure themselves that if they had worked, they could have passed. Others may be so confused about whether or not they feel they can separate from their parents that they opt out of university altogether.

Georgina, seventeen, was so angry with her parents and her school for pressuring her to go to a prestigious university to do medicine that she rebelled against both in a way that was ultimately very self-destructive. Her behaviour also demonstrated her real fears about leaving the familiar world of home and school for the unknown world of university.

In her last term at school, just before taking her 'A' level exams, Georgina suddenly announced that she no longer wanted to go to university. She told her parents that instead she was going to go round the world with her musician boyfriend, whom she had known since she was at primary school. Nothing anyone could say would make her change her mind and eventually, against all advice, she left school and went off with her boyfriend to establish her own identity, separate from the wishes of her teachers and parents.

Superficially she was taking a stand against parental and school pressure but deep down, she was also clinging to the known and the familiar in the form of her long-standing boyfriend. Georgina was exceptionally bright but she came from a working class background with no tradition of going to university and she was frightened of what the next step would mean. Additionally, her transition to secondary school had been difficult because she was bright and had been bullied by other pupils. The prospect of going to university stirred up memories of this painful experience.

MIXED FEELINGS 4   HOW WILL I GET TO KNOW ANYONE? WILL ANYONE LIKE ME OR REMEMBER ME?

A further anxiety about universities has to do with their sheer size. Some have as many as twenty-five to thirty thousand students, so young people entering them are moving into a very big pond indeed, especially when their school may have had no more than a thousand pupils. They will experience different, less intimate relationships with lecturers, and very different ways of studying.

Some young people may resolve their anxieties about not having friends by 'grabbing' at the first person who smiles at them, without taking the time to find out who that person is, whether he or she can be trusted or whether they actually like them.

"When I was at school, I knew everyone and everyone knew me. We all lived near each other. Some of the people I did 'A' levels with were at primary school with me. When I first came to university, I felt completely

lost. No-one from my school came to this university and I couldn't seem to remember how to make new friends. In the end I got stuck with someone I didn't really like, just because she was nice to me. I wish I had waited and been more choosey."   Marianne, 1st year Business Studies student

"I hate where I am living. No-one ever does the washing-up, or the cleaning. They just seem to leave it to me. When I had to leave halls at the end of the first year, I panicked that no one would want to share a flat with me. When someone in my lectures said they needed an extra flatmate, I just agreed without thinking. They all know each other and I don't feel I belong."   Ben, 2nd year French student

Other young people may 'resolve' the friendship question by maintaining romantic relationships from home long past their 'sell-by date', and not take the risk of entering new relationships. Or they may avoid the issue altogether by burying themselves in their work or their rooms (*see below*).

MIXED FEELINGS 5   WHAT WILL I EAT?

Although the majority of young people who are fortunate enough to go to university away from home really look forward to living on their own with their peers, they can also be anxious about very basic things, like looking after themselves. Many of them have never cooked for themselves or done their own washing, cleaning and shopping. They have reached a status, in the sheltered environment of school, where they are looked up to by younger pupils and they have the illusion of being grown up. However, in reality, many of them still feel like children in terms of day-to-day existence. Rather like the toddler who can only run away from his mother in the park if he is sure she will be there when he returns, young people still need parents and teachers in the background to help them make the transition to independent living.

James had been at university for six weeks before phoning his father to say, "I'm getting really sick of tuna, what should I do?" He had no idea how to cook and had been eating tuna every day since he arrived. "Have you thought of eggs?" asked his father. "That's a good idea," said the student and put the phone down. This student only needed his father at the other end of the phone, to give him an idea of what to eat, and then he could get on with being a student.

Anxieties about being able to look after oneself can trigger ancient insecurities for young people who as children, experienced neglect from their primary carer. If they - literally - don't know where their next meal is coming from, old insecurities about never having enough may provoke painful and primitive feelings of deprivation completely disproportionate to their here-and-now experience.

MIXED FEELINGS 6   WILL MY FAMILY BE OK?

James was a pretty self-sufficient young man, who came from a secure base, whose parents were happy to give him a bit of support when he needed it. Because of this, he could really use the transitional space to develop and become independent. However, some students may not feel they are in a position to use university in this way because they have responsibilities at home which make this very difficult. They may have been looking after younger brothers and sisters for years, and they may be quite experienced at looking after themselves. They may come from single parent families where they have taken up a caretaker role, and they may worry how their families will manage without them once they reach university.

Mike came to see a counsellor only a couple of weeks after arriving at university, to say he was considering dropping out. His father had left home when he was eleven and Mike had taken his father's place, looking after his depressed mother, younger brother and two sisters. He felt immensely guilty for pursuing his own career as an engineer, when his mother was struggling at home looking after his younger siblings. He absolutely loved the course, and this increased his feeling of guilt. For him, separating from the family in general and his mother in particular was a very painful experience and he wasn't sure if he could attach himself to the university sufficiently to make the developmental move he needed to get on with his own life and his own career.

MIXED FEELINGS 7   HOW WILL I KNOW HOW TO SPEND MY TIME? HOW WILL I KNOW WHAT IS ENOUGH?

This young man had sacrificed part of his development to support his mother and now he was considering sacrificing his future as well. Other students, with easier and more straight-forward home situations may struggle with the freedom that university brings when they no longer have parents and teachers telling them what to do.

Universities have very different expectations of their students than schools do. They expect their students to be self-motivated in their learning; the whole educational experience is far less structured than it is at school. Young people may have considered themselves terribly grown-up at school, because they behaved in quite a rebellious way within the safe confines of home and school. But they may find it quite confusing when no-one is there to object if they come home late or don't come in at all. They may find the apparent lack of structure at university disconcerting. If they only have lectures on two or three days, and don't have a job, they may wonder what to do with the rest of the week. In theory, they may welcome the fact that no-one checks whether they attend lectures or not. But deep down, it might come as quite a shock that nobody tells them off if they don't hand an essay in on time, and they simply fail that piece of work.

They may experience this new-found freedom as a lack of concern on the part of their lecturers. They may miss the teachers who knew them well and kept them on their toes. Young people with attachment difficulties especially may feel the lack of the consistency of relationship provided by a particular teacher who was interested and involved in their development. It can be upsetting to students that no-one is there to remind them not to go to bed too late, even if they used to resent such input. If they feel too tired to study or to work the next day, if they drink too much or take drugs, they will have to consider for themselves how this will affect their work, their health and their life. Such erratic habits can create a mental milieu for young people with attachment difficulties in which old sensitivities, to loss, sudden changes, and 'trigger' situations which carry a reminder of old threats, can be exacerbated.

Without the security that external boundaries and expectations provided, without consistency of relationship, these students may experience strong feelings of anxiety and uncertainty, and feel that no-one is 'holding them in mind'. Their earlier behaviour patterns may surface in response to this anxiety. Their behaviour and responses may seem strange or weird to other students from more settled backgrounds, and this may reinforce the young person's difficulty with making friends, leaving them feeling yet more isolated (*and see* Chapter 1, p.21).

Students with an insecure avoidant attachment pattern may avoid the need to connect socially with other students or deal with tutors. They may focus exclusively on their studies and become perfectionist about their work, shutting themselves away in their rooms or libraries, or spending inordinate amounts of time on the internet. Their problems may only come to light very late in their time at university, when the strain of academic pressures escalates. Students with an insecure ambivalent attachment pattern of behaviour may cling to a friend or group of friends, and neglect to separate out to get on with their studies independently. They may experience great anxiety when academic demands mean they need to spend time working alone, and be unable to complete their assignments. Their ability to research, take in and think about new information will be compromised.

Some students may manage their anxiety and insecurity through more and more extreme behaviour, which could eventually bring them containment through confrontation with university authorities or the law. Their behaviour will bring them out of the anonymity of being an unnamed student into some kind of relationship with tutors, deans, administrators or the police, just as at school they might have 'engineered' getting themselves put on report (*see* Chapter 2). Alternatively, they may use alcohol, drugs, sex, gambling or their relationship to food to numb out their distressing feelings.

Peter, a mature student who came to university with a history of mental health and alcohol problems, was disciplined in the period leading up to the exams. One day he had come into a lecture theatre drunk, and shouted out that the lecture was boring and the lecturer was useless. In fact, he was terrified that he would be thrown out of university if he failed the exams and was projecting his inadequacy onto the lecturer, who was actually someone he admired and envied. His alcohol problems and his insecure attachment meant that instead of asking for help, he became aggressive and rude when he was anxious. He was eventually given a warning that if he ever behaved that way again, he would be excluded. Fortunately until the exam period, he had managed to contain his drinking problem at a social level. The pressure of exams pushed his problems to the forefront.

MIXED FEELINGS 8   WILL I BE ABLE TO MANAGE FINANCIALLY?
CAN I REALLY BE INDEPENDENT?

Although we have seen that university can be a place where adolescents learn to be independent and grow up, this is complicated by the fact that most students are still financially dependent, at least in part, on their parents. This can get in the way of them feeling they can properly separate. Many students also have to work to make ends meet and this can put a strain on them. Students whose parents have never encouraged them to practise managing their money, and who are unready to give up this dependent aspect of their relationship, may run up huge debts, expecting to be 'bailed out'. Others may be lulled into believing that becoming bankrupt is 'not that big a deal'. Both these latter stances indicate a lack of willingness to engage with the real world, and perhaps indicate an anxiety about the separation from their families that financial independence and responsibility implies.

For students living at home, attaching to the university requires extra effort, and some students may prefer to stay with their familiar friends, go to their old haunts and lead a life that is really an extension of school.

One such young woman was A'noud, who reached her final year and felt she has missed out on being a student. She had worked in her father's shop most evenings and most weekends, and came to the counselling service when she realised that the next step her parents has planned for her was marriage. She had seen her peers having fun and making relationships but she felt he should not be doing this. She was faced with a clash of cultures, one at home and one at university, and she was beginning to wish she had joined in and become more involved the social life.

Until her final year, A'noud had been getting very good marks on her course, but now her work was deteriorating and she was in danger of failing her final year. Unconsciously, her adolescent protest against the conformity she had willingly adopted was taking the form of a self-destructive attack on the one thing she really wanted to do, which was to become a lawyer. Like many young people in the newer universities, A'noud was the first in her family to go to university. She hadn't known what to expect and it was only in her final year that she realised she had missed out on using it as a transitional space to establish her independence.

Helping young people make the transition to university

We can see from the examples in this chapter, that when young people make the transition from school to university, they face similar emotional struggles to younger children making earlier educational transitions. Each stage is a step nearer to adult independence and each step can be facilitated or assisted by the tactful support of parents and teachers.

How can schools help?

Schools can play an extremely valuable part in helping prepare young people for the challenges and opportunities ahead. Some schools, like the Academy described above, arrange discussions workshops to prepare young people for university. In such groups staff can

- ✓ Invite students to express their hopes and fears and talk about the issues discussed above

- ✓ Normalise the range of feelings students may experience in the critical first term of university (when the drop-out rate is at its highest)

- ✓ Help students build resilience by looking back at how they have already coped with difficult transitions in the past, and helping them remember what coping strategies have worked before and could work again at university

- ✓ Discuss or role-play new coping strategies relevant to the student's concerns

- ✓ Normalise the need to seek help from time to time, and help students become familiar with the range of support available at university (Student Counselling Service, student support, health and welfare services, Helplines, CAB and so on)

- ✓ Involve student counsellors from universities, to help facilitate the discussion, to describe the work of the student counselling service and to allow the young people to 'put a human face' on the counselling relationship

✓ Invite ex-pupils now at university back to the school to talk to those wanting to apply, giving them a tangible sense of what the experience is like, and what helped them settle in

How can universities help?

Universities need to offer students a 'secure base' if they genuinely wish to help them form an attachment to the place, the people and their studies, especially in the crucial first term. Many universities have programmes, such as e-mentoring, buddy schemes, parent and student inductions, group tutorials and welcome programmes to ensure that new students are helped with some of the issues discussed in this chapter. A college at one university has a 'parenting' scheme in which second year students befriend a new student for the first three days of their time at university, and are subsequently available as and when they are needed in the next few weeks.

✓ Everyone working in universities should be aware of how important the transition into university is for students, and how anxious they can feel when they first arrive

✓ Systems need to be in place to make them feel welcome. For example, there should be notices that tell them where to go for each activity; staff from receptionists to registry staff should be welcoming and friendly; there should be welcome programmes and inductions and social activities that are relevant and interesting. Halls of Residence staff in particular should be sensitive to how new students might be feeling and provide welcoming activities to help students feel at home

✓ The university website should be highly accessible, with links to key student support services (especially the Student Counselling Service) clearly available on the home page

- ✔ Institutional chaos, at the beginning of the year, can add to a sense of not belonging, especially for students with insecure attachment patterns. Staff should be aware that students are at the highest risk of dropping out in the first twelve weeks of their first year at university

- ✔ Universities need tutorial policies and tutorial systems that allow students to engage with their lecturers from day one. Students should be introduced to their tutors as early as possible, so that each student is known to someone within the university as soon as they arrive

- ✔ Departments should have a strong and visible commitment to student well-being

- ✔ Counselling and other student services should be welcoming and high profile, both personally and through publicity, especially during the first few weeks of term. In universities where induction programmes could be improved, counsellors should be lobbying for this and explaining why it is so important. Counselling services should put on workshops about making the transition into university, to highlight the normal feelings that can arise at this time

- ✔ Widening Participation and increased student numbers have brought in many students who have never had the opportunity to go to university before. Staff should have training in adjusting to the different needs of these students. There may be a culture clash between students and academics about what higher education is about. Academic staff and Counselling Services need to work together on this

- ✔ Mentoring and E Mentoring schemes may be useful ways of engaging students in a relationship and ensuring that they don't fall by the wayside. Counsellors may be useful in training students in these schemes, and also in setting up buddy schemes in which second or third year students befriend a new student while he or she settles into university

✔ Universities should pay particular attention to the needs of more
    vulnerable students. Their duty of care, under the Disability
    Discrimination Act, means that these students should be provided with
    reasonable adjustment as well as the support they need to get them
    through their studies

Conclusion

We have seen the challenges students face in the move from school to university,
especially those students who have previously had difficult transitions or who
experience attachment difficulties. To do justice to their struggle, and to help them
make the most of the opportunity they have earned for themselves, it is critical that
schools and universities, like nurseries, primary and secondary schools, understand
what young people are going through when they make this major transition, and do
everything they can to support them. Marris (1974) quotes John Bowlby,

> First the child, then the adolescent, and finally the young adult moves out
> in a series of ever-lengthening excursions… each step follows the previous
> one in a series of easy stages. Though home ties may attenuate, they are
> never broken.   Bowlby 1970, in Marris 1974 p.19

Marris then goes on to say,

> Thus the self-confidence of maturity is not a rejection of support, but an
> ability to turn for reassurance when need arises, trusting that it will be
> met. The confirmation that more primitive wants are securely satisfied
> renews confidence to confront the uncertainties of growth. Conversely, if
> these wants have never been fully met, growing up does indeed become
> a succession of bereavements; the grown person is a banished child with
> forged papers of maturity.   (p.20)

In summary

- Going to university is potentially one of the most exciting times in a young person's life. It provides them with a transitional space, or intermediate zone between home and the real world, in which they can separate from their parents and prepare for an independent life

- This transitional space brings with it exciting new challenges and opportunities, but it also arouses fears and anxieties, especially for the increasing numbers of students entering university from a diverse range of backgrounds and abilities, including refugees and international students

- For all young people, going to university stirs up memories of earlier transitions. If these experiences have been difficult or complicated, it will affect the way they able to attach to university and be successful students. Students with attachment difficulties who have had traumatic experiences of separation and loss, as a result of bereavement, abuse, or neglect, may be particularly vulnerable

- Moving from school to university can feel like moving from being a big fish in a small pond to being a tiny fish in a much bigger pond. In some cases, this leads to feelings of isolation, underachievement and psychological problems. In more extreme cases it can lead to alcohol and drug abuse, eating problems, acting out or serious depression, suicidal thoughts, panic attacks and other mental health problems

(continues ...)

- Schools can do an enormous amount to support students as they prepare to make the transition, especially those students with known attachment difficulties. All time spent in preparation will pay dividends in helping students make the attachment to university

- Universities need to be aware of potential attachment issues for all students and provide comprehensive welcome programmes, induction programmes, social activities and tutorial, counselling and healthcare support for all students. They should also pay particular attention to the needs of the more vulnerable students, especially during the critical first twelve weeks/first term. Their duty of care, under the Disability Discrimination Act, means that these students should be provided with reasonable adjustments as well as the support they need to get them through their courses, and make the most of everything on offer at university as an important gateway to adult life

References

Abram, J. (1996) *The Language of Winnicott: A dictionary of Winnicott's use of words*
London: Karnac Books

Department for Education and Skills (DfES) publication, *Widening Participation in Higher Education*,
London 2003

Geddes, H. (2003) *Attachment in the Classroom: The links between children's early experience,
emotional well-being and performance in school* London: Worth Publishing

Marris, P. (1974) *Loss and Change* London: Routledge & Kegan Paul

Rana, R. (2000) *Counselling Students: A psychodynamic perspective* London: Macmillan Press Ltd

Winnicott, D.W. (1964) *The Child, the Family and the Outside World*
Harmondsworth: Penguin Books
Winnicott, D. W. (1971) *Playing and Reality* London: Tavistock Publications

Index

A

abuse 2, 16, 25, 31, 66, 84,
123-4, 178-9
academic: *ability*, 202:
achievement, 20, 24, 206, 207: *mid-a.year*, 36, 113: *performance*, 22:
pressure, 212: *problems*, 19: *task*,
199: *work*, 149, 163,
169, 196
acceptance 6, 17, 41, 101,
110, 126, 129
addicted parents 24
addiction 15, 79, 189, 201
adoption 16: *adoptive culture*, 165:
adoptive parents, 16, 47, 198
**ambivalent attachment 11, 20,
79-83:** *within groups*, 17
aggressive behaviour 10, 11, 15, 17,
20, 65, 85, 89, 91, 107, 200, 213,
179: *aggression-rejection pattern*,
15: *as form of attachment*, 14, 18:
non-, 177
anger 4, 10, 91, 97, 107, 131,
161, 207: *management*, 98, 106,
109, 131
anxiety 4, 9, 14, 18, 19, 21, 23,
24, 25, 51, 52, 54, 56, 69, 76, 78, 80,
82, 85, 91, 103, 105, 106,
109, 114, 159, 168, 177, 202,
205, 208, 212, 213, 214: *separation
-*, 14
art 94, 99, 105, **109:** *creative arts*, 6,
142, 154, 155, **160-163, 169:** *use of
in forming attachment relationship*,
99-112, 186

attachment: *Adult Attachment
Interview*, 12: *authentic a. -
relationship*, **97-118:** *behaviour:* 5,
7, 10, 12, 82: *bonds*, 150: *difficulties*,
3, 4, 6, 7, **9-26,** 31, 32, 33, 36, 41,
46, 47, 50, 51, 53, 54, 57, 90, 99,
103, 105, 197, 198, 199, 201, 203,
204, 212, 218: *development of*, 9:
disorders, **12-23:** *figure*, 4, 9, 10,
11, 14, 16, 20, 98, 100, 101, 125,
176, 180: *and groups*, **16-26:** *and
hope*, 175: *impoverished*, 177: *losses*,
142: *needs*, 11, 179: *of the streets*,
180-1: *patterns*, 3, 10, 11, 20, 21,
69-92, 102, 107, 142, 150-2, 158,
169, 200, 212, 217: *perspective*, 5,
6, 68, 88: *positive -* , 5, 7: *profile*, 3:
relationship: 9, **97-118, 123-139:** *to
homeland*, 142: *safe -* , 26: *styles*, 93,
94: *system*, 10, 22, 176
Attachment Theory 9, 64, 112
attune, attunement 126, 129, 136,
137, 153, 154, 201: *mis -* , 110
avoidant attachment 7, 11, 17, 20,
41, **60-78,** 106, 113, 212

B

beginnings 31
behaviour *challenging*, 2, 3, 4, 41, 84,
103, 181, 185: *as communication*
3, 34, 58, **93,** 107, 118: *risky*, 13, 18,
84, 181, 189
belonging 18, 41, **152,** 156-7, 199,
217

behaviour management strategies
2, 63, 67, 68: *assumptions
underpinning*, **88-9**
blame, blaming 51, 81, 87, 95
boundary, boundaries 13, 22, 52,
80, 87, 93, 105, 108, 114, 145, 154,
160, 166, 187, 212
Bowlby, J. 3, 9, 10, 38, 150, 152, 218
brain 151, 176, 178: *collective brain*,
120: *growth*, 42, 53: *left brain*, 74,
83, 88, 94
bullying 85, 179, 208

C

CAMHS 106, 113, 149, 151, 163, 169
challenging behaviour see behaviour
choice 46, 73, 77, 89, 97, 104, 108,
158, 207: *of key adult*, 39, 101:
of language & behaviour, 56
chronological age 32, 40, 52, 86, 89,
105
circle time 91
**classification of attachment
disorders,** 12
clay 161, **162**
clinging 10-14, 80, 207, 208, 212
commentaries 49, 94, 111
communication *attunement as
component of*, 129: *behaviour as*,
see behaviour: *genuine*, 101: *in
metaphor*, 161: *non-verbal*, 100:
'nourishing', 105
conflict 1, 11, 20, 21, 57, 106, 126,
127, 153, 201: *developmental*, 206

consistency 5, 34, 38, 39, 43, 53, 54, 58, 68, **75**, 85, 102, 116, 212

contain, containing, containment 4, 19, 54, 56, 87, 100, 101, 108, 151, 154, 157, 159, 161, 200, 201, 202, 213: *uncontaining,* 199

continuing professional development **53**

continuity **33**, 44, **47**

control 89, 92, 123, 127, 150, 183, 190: *battles,* 47, **76-78**: *of activity,* 73: *of feelings,* 48: *of lesson,* 66: *of proximity to others,* 102: *of self,* 75: *of weight,* 25

counselling 5, 86, 114, 200, 204: *student c. - service,* 153, 202, 204, 214, **215-8**: *school counsellors,* 54, 204: *university counsellors,* 201, 204, 206

counter-transference 185

creative arts, *see art, creative*

creativity 94, 97, **99**, 186

curiosity 6, 10, 19, 41, 94, 126

D

defence mechanisms 38, 51, 75, 77, 93, 98, 105, 106, 108, 113

dependency 21, 40, 50, 100

developmental *age,* 50, 53: *conflict,* 206: *issue,* 159: *need,* 110, 159: *stage,* 34, 36, 48, 89, 200, 211: *task,* 197: *vulnerability,* 31, 33, **53**

differentiate, differentiation 6, 53, 94, 103, 111, 112

dignity 8, **55-6**, 99, 108, 181, 191

disorganised attachment 11, **15**, 21, **83-8**, 102

disinhibited attachment behaviour 12, 13, 18

drama 74, 91, 92, 94, 161

drugs 6, 24, 179, **180-1**, 199, 200, 212: *drug culture,* 61: *drug dealer,* 76, 177, 179, 189

dyslexia 98, 198

dys-regulation 154, 178, 187

E

eating *disorder,* 15, 18, 25, 182, 219

educational *aims,* 158: *band-aid,* 98: *experience,* 211: *groups,* 142: *psychologist,* 86, 106, 200: *psychotherapist,* 3, 64: *setting,* 202: *staff,* 3, 57, 200: *transitions,* **31-60**, 203, 215:

emotions 4, 21, 77, 118, 129, 147, 150, 154, 157, 161, 162, 178, 183, 184, 187, 201

emotional *age,* 32, 36, 53, 86, 90, 97, 101, 105: *arousal,* 148: *attachment,* 9, 10, 22: *availability,* 19, 70, 80: *centres of the brain,* 178: *commitment,* 20: *development,* 89, 97, 200: *difficulties,* 186, 202: *disorder,* 13: *distress,* 100: *energy,* 81: *environment,* 16: *expectations,* 53: *expression,* 127: *growth,* 33: *health,* 46, 54, 94, 103, 118, 153, 187: *impact,* 36: *intelligence,* 162: *life,* 176: *literacy,* 46, 116: *management,* 187: *maturity,* 101: *presence,* 21: *problems,* 123: *relationship,* 17: *needs,* 94, 100, 106, 112, 114: *reserves,* 36: *response,* 148: *safe haven,* 11, 16: *scaffolding,* 41: *secure base,* **39**: *security,* 16: *skills,* 94: *state,* 126, 154: *stress,* 10: *struggle,* 215: *support,* 18, 19, 20

empathic attunement 154

empathy 6, 86, 96, 98, 116, 125, 126, 137, 176

endings 45-7, 87

exclusion 2, 4, 32, 35, 36, **38**, 45, 55, 76, 92, 123, 181, 186, 198

F

failure 21, 52, 93, 98, 128, 137, 148, 176, 184, 207

father 10, 12, 15, 24, 76, 84, 141, 176, 200, 210: *fatherless,* 142

feral 2, 175

fresh starts **33**, 43

friends 19, 21, 22, 24, 67, 73, 113, 114, 128, 130, 136, 141, 196, 203, 205, 208, 209, 212, 214, 216, 218

frustration 4, 56, 69, 82, 85, 98, 107, 116, 206

fun 7, 69, 105, 115, 160, 188, 196: *making time for,* **42**

G, H

games 91, 92, 94, 103, 104, 160, 207

Geddes, H. **3**, 4, 72, 81, 105, 199

good enough 32, 34, 36, 40, 206, 214

grief 87, 147, **149-50**, 159, 161

group 12, 47, 73, 103, **140-170**, 204: *approach,* 6: *attachment to,* 9, **16-26**: *behaviour in,* 20, 21, 89, 164: *peer group, see peer: meaning to refugees,* 152-4

'hold in mind', 'keep in mind' 4, 7, 32, 39, 40, 41, 49, 79, 80, 82, 112, 115, 152, 190, 212

home 14, 52, 106, 144, **151-3**, 155, 162, 165, 177, 179, 182, 194, 196-8, 200, 203, 205, 207, 211, 214, 218: *country,* 158: *foster,* 22, 123-4, 169: *homeland,* 142, 153: *homelessness,* 186, 197: *homesick,* 149, 197: *H-Office,* 144, 169, 186: *violence in,* 24

home/school partnership 51

hoodie 2, 174

hope 2, 7, 37, 45, 52, 139, 143, 151, 157, 165, 170, 175, 187, 198, 203, 204, 215

humiliation 55, 177, 179, 185

hyper-vigilance 35, 79, 85, 146-7

I

inclusion 38-9, 50, 101, 117

independence 7, 50, 82, 88, 126, 196, 197, 205, 214, 215

inhibited attachment 12, 13, 14, 17

insecure attachment 2-4, **10-17**, 20, 21, 34, 38, **69-88**, 106, 151, 200, 212, 213, 217

Institute for Arts in Therapy & Education (IATE) 109

intentions *adolescent's,* 125, 125: *adults,* 97, 99, 127, 136, 178: *joint,* 128, 136

interpretation 57, 111, 129, 139, 183

interpreters 142, 155, 158, 159, 163, 164, **165**, 167

intersubjectivity 6, **123-139**

K, L

'keep in mind' *see 'hold in mind'*
key adult 4, 34, 38, 39, **40-1**, 44, 47, 48, 49, 51, 52, 53, 55, 56, 80, 103, 105, 106-7, 114-6, 183, 184
key worker 4, 39, 48, 98, 99: *as attachment figure*, **101-18, 183**
Kids' Company 175, 181, 185, **186**
language, use of positive 52, 54, **56-7**, 77, 91, 94, 127
Learning Triangle 3, 72, 81, 85, 199
leaving *home*, 195, 207: *school*, 4, 87, 197, 206: *teaching*, 4: *university*, 195
loss 1, 2, 3, 12, 14, 31, 32, 33, 35, 36, 42, 44, 47, 53, 54, 57, 142, 157, 161, 190, 198, 201, 206, 212

M, N

meetings 43, **53-4**, 83, 88, 91, 193, 104, 109, 124, 127, 146, 167
mental health, 46, **54-5**, 152, 155, 176: *difficulties*, 35, 198, 201: *professionals*, 168: *services*, 2, 151, 200, 213: *state*, 68
mentors 39, 67, 87, 88, 91, 92, 93, 101, 114, 123, 126, 129, 163, 218: *e-mentor*, 216, 218: *peer*, 83, 113: *SAFE®*, 26
metaphor 73, 74, 94, 161, 182
mother 10, 11, 15, 18, 24, 76, 79, 84, 100, 112, 141, 142, 149, 150, **152, 176-7**, 188, 200, 202, 209, 211: *motherless*, 142
neglect 2, 10, 16, 31, 50, 84, 178, 198, 210

O, P

observation 34, 93, 113, 117, 145, 163
omnipotence **77**
PACE 126
peers 9, 13, 32, 36, 37, 46, 47, 52, 73, 75, 76, 82, 84, 85, 86, 103, 114, 145, 146, 155, 163, 165, 179, 181, 199, 209, 214: *group*, 16-19, 21, 23, 31, 50, 114, 149, 206
play 13, 42, 91, 94, 105, 154, 160, **162**: *playfulness*, 6, 14, 126, 207: *sand -*, 190

positive expectations 45, 52, 54, 94, 203
post-traumatic stress disorder (PTSD) **147-9**
potential 4, 21, 33, 200, 206
projection 2, 14, 18, 107, 213
promiscuous attachment behaviour 13, 18, 22
psychosomatic 15, 19

R

reading 53: *age*, 106: *recovery*, 98
reflection 3, 5, 32, 34-5, 46, 53, 87, 88, 101, 108, 113, 116, 157, **163**
refugee 6, **140-170**
rejection 14, 15, 32, 67, 71, 73, 106-7, 111, 116, 137, 180, 190, 197, 207
resilience 10, 118, 142, 150, 154, 177, 185, 215
respect 7, 20, 44, 53, 86, 90, 100, 102, 105, 113, 114, 125, 129, 152, 154, 158, 160, 166, 190, 203
risk taking in learning 39, 69, 76, 137, 190, 209
risky *behaviour see* behaviour as *core aspect of adolescence*, 188
role reversal 15, 18, 24
rules 87, 107, 128, 131, 145, 154, 161, 166, 175, 203

S

SAFE® programme 26
scaffolding 41
school community 103
school phobia 14
second-chance learning 4, 40 57
secure *attachment*, 5, 10, 18, 19, 20, 26, 151: *in groups*, **16, 152**
secure base 5, 6, 15, 16, 24, 34, **38-42**, 77, 87, 90, 101, 108, 142, 198, 210, 216: *group as*, **151-61**
self *assessment*, 196: *awareness*, 157: *banishment*, 180: *belief*, 143: *confidence*, 218: *destructive behaviour*, 107, 214: *direction*, 73, 109, 110: *disgust*, 178, 179: *esteem*, 21, 68, 186, 190: *expression*,

108, 111: *harm*, 65, 71, 189: *management*, 44, 56: *medication*, 199, 200: *regulation*, 154-5, 160, **183**, 196: *revelation*, 161: *soothing*, 154, 176: *validation*, 157
SENCO 5, 101, 154
separation 9, 11-14, 16, 19, 25, 81, 82, 177, **195-8**, 201, 205, 207: *anxiety*, 14
shame 55, 98, 126, 156: *toxic*, **56**
shouting 22, 55, 67, 213
splitting 21, 51, 75
stress 4, 11, 16, 42, 118, 126, 142, 151, 154, 156, 158: *emotional*, 10: *hormones*, 42, 177: *response*, 44, 55: *staff*, 4, 67-8, 143

T

Team Around the Child (TAC) 34, **54**
therapeutic team 102, 183
transitional space 196, 210, 214
transitions 6, **31-58**, 87, 160, **195-218**
trauma 2, 3, 5, 7, 10, 12, 15, 26, 31, 54, 106, 112, 125, 145, 147, 148, 154, **156**, 157, 160, 180, 183, 185, 187, 192, 198, 201, 206: *traumatic*, 12, 23, 25, 32, 45, 142, **147**, 151, 157, 158, 161, 183
triggers *of extreme behaviour*, 15, 84, 178: *of feelings*, 159: *of insecurity*, 210: *of memory*, 15: *of panic*, 22, **44**, 212
truant, truanting 85

U, V, W

unaccompanied minor 6, **144**, 155, 166
undifferentiated attachment behaviour 13
university 3, 7, 76, **195-218**
violence 6, 12, 21-6, 79, 84, 164, 175, 179, 189, 190, 200: *adolescents'*, **176-9**: *domestic*, 2, 14, 16, 88, 177, 201: *role of*, **180-1**
Widening Participation 198, 217
wondering aloud 92